The Jesus Diet

How Jesus said to overcome weakness, sickness, and premature death

Terry Toler

The Jesus Diet

Published by: BeHoldings, LLC.
Copyright ©2020, **BeHoldings, LLC**
Terrytoler.com.
All Rights Reserved

Cover and interior designs: BeHoldings, LLC.

Our books can be purchased in bulk for promotional, educational and business use. Please contact your bookseller or the BeHoldings Publishing Sales department at: sales@terrytoler.com

For booking information email: booking@terrytoler.com:

First U.S. Edition: October 2020
Printed in the United States of America
ISBN: 978-1-7352243-8-1

ABOUT THE AUTHOR

Terry Toler is the author of numerous books on success in the areas of marriage, health, and finance all centered around a relationship with Jesus Christ and several fiction books. Terry has been a motivational speaker and success counselor for more than thirty years and has helped thousands set goals for their life and then achieve them. Terry and his wife, Donna, live in Arkansas where they live out the principles of The Jesus Diet every day.

This book is dedicated to the reader.
Divine health is a right for every Christian.
My prayer is that this book will help you start your journey
to divine health or help to improve your health
if you are already on the journey.

PLEASE READ BEFORE BEGINNING THIS BOOK

This is a faith-based book. The intention is not for it to offer or take the place of medical advice. Do not rely on it for the treatment or diagnosis of any medical condition. Please consult your health care provider for medical questions.

BOOKS BY TERRY TOLER

How to Make More Than a Million Dollars
The Heart Attacked
Seven Years of Promise
Mission Possible
Marriage Made in Heaven
21 Days to Physical Healing
21 Days to Spiritual Fitness
21 Days to Divine Health
21 Days to a Great Marriage
21 Days to Financial Freedom
21 Days to Sharing Your Faith
21 Days to Mission Possible
7 Days to Emotional Freedom
Uncommon Finances
Suddenly Free

Fiction Books

The Longest Day
The Reformation of Mars
The Great Wall of Ven-Us
The Eden Experiment
The Late, Great Planet Jupiter
Save The Girls
The Ingenue
The Blue Rose

For more information on these books and other resources
visit TerryToler.com.

THE JESUS DIET
CONTENTS

INTRODUCTION

In the beginning was the Word, and the Word was with God, and
the Word was God. He was in the beginning with God. All things
were made through Him, and without Him nothing was made that
was made. (John 1:1–3)

Everything in this book begins with Jesus. For that matter, everything pertaining to life started with Jesus. When John said that the
Word was in the beginning and nothing was made without Him, he
was talking about Jesus. Jesus said He came to this earth to provide
us with eternal life and abundant life. We will someday live in
heaven because of Jesus. That is eternal life. However, abundant life
is here on earth. The word "abundant" means exceedingly good. It's
very difficult to have an exceedingly abundant life apart from good
health.

If you don't feel physically well, you probably don't think you
have an abundant life. If you don't have abundant life in health,
there must be a reason for this since it is promised to you. I'm convinced that if I am going to be healthy, it will be because of Jesus.
Freedom from sickness and disease is all because of His finished
works on the cross.

Do you believe that? I don't know why you picked up this book,
but it is probably related to some health issue or some desire to improve your health. Maybe you or someone you know is suffering
from:

- Addiction
- Anxiety

- Panic Attacks
- Fear
- Obesity
- Chronic Pain
- Sorrow
- Eating Disorders
- Heart Disease
- Cancer
- Diabetes
- Abuse

If anyone is ever to overcome their health issues, it will be because of what Jesus has done for him in the new covenant of grace.

Throughout this book, I will reference the old covenant and the new covenant. In the old covenant, there were 613 laws, rules, and regulations that had to be followed to be in good standing with God and to be healthy. In the new covenant of grace, all that is needed is simply to believe in Jesus and profess Him as your Lord.

That is the fundamental principle of this book. You are saved by Jesus, and your health is transformed by Jesus. He is the key to everything. He's the key to a fulfilling marriage. He's the key to financial prosperity. He's the key to health, weight loss, and a life free from sickness and disease. Divine health begins with Him.

The principles of the Jesus Diet are found in the teachings of Jesus. Most people don't realize how much Jesus talked about food and drink. You're going to find that the principles are really very simple and much easier to follow than the old covenant dietary laws. They are much more effective than today's diet plans that don't work and are nearly impossible to follow. Mark Twain said, "The only way to keep your health is to eat what you don't want, drink what you don't like, and do what you'd druther not." Have you ever felt that way? There's a better way. You're not going to believe how simple the Jesus Diet really is. Since the new covenant of grace is accessed by believing in Jesus, you're going to have to believe, or it won't work for you!

It is a benefit to us that good health is a part of grace, because, truthfully, we don't deserve health and wellness. If we look at the average American diet, we will realize we deserve to be overweight, sick, weak, and to die prematurely. The first man, Adam, lived 930 years! Your body was created to live a lot longer than you will actually live. Because of sin and our diet, the average lifespan is now seventy-two years!

We didn't create all our health problems. Some of them are environmental. Some are genetic and hereditary. Sometimes, our bodies work against us, and some problems we bring on ourselves. Regardless of why we are unhealthy, God has provided grace through Jesus to resolve every health problem. In this book, you're going to discover how to access His grace. These principles can transform your health once and for all. Don't misunderstand. I don't have any power to transform your life. This book has no power to change your health, but Jesus does, and He wants to through His grace and truth.

The Bible has an interesting story about two brothers who were constantly fighting. Esau was the oldest and came home one day from hunting to find his brother, Jacob, making stew. Esau was exhausted and starving, desperate for a meal. He asked his brother for a bite, and Jacob said he would give him some if he sold him his birthright. Jacob was totally out of line, but Esau literally gave up his entire birthright for that one meal! The Bible says Esau was so distraught that he "despised" his birthright. Hebrews 12 says Esau was godless and lost his blessing with tears.

Food is the source of a lot of pain for a lot of people. Even though they hunger for it they eat it, and then regret it, maybe not immediately, but certainly over time when their health begins to deteriorate. It's a vicious cycle. Have you ever cried because of your health situation? You're going to learn through this book why you have a love/hate relationship with food and how to get out of that cycle once and for all.

If you struggle with your weight, you're going to discover how to lose those extra pounds. If you're sick, the Jesus Diet will help you. If you just want to be healthier, you'll find some answers here. You're going to learn how Jesus can set you free from a life-long struggle to achieve health and wellness. It will not be through your self-effort or obedience to a set of laws and regulations. That is the old covenant. Those haven't worked anyway. It'll be through the finished works of Christ on the cross. Jesus is going to do it. That is the new covenant of grace.

The Jesus Diet has dramatically changed my life and is continuing to change my health every day. You are just a few chapters away from experiencing a health transformation that you never thought was possible. Let's begin the journey.

PART ONE

RECEIVE FOOD WITH THANKSGIVING

CHAPTER 1
LIVE FREE OR DIET

Are you tired of hearing the word "diet"? I know I am. On any given day, some forty-five million Americans are on one. Women tend to diet more than men and as many as forty-five percent of women are dieting at any given time. Hundreds of diets promise instant results and guaranteed weight loss, but few deliver on that promise. They not only don't work but are confusing and often contradict each other. Some studies say that a high-protein, low-carbohydrate diet is the way to go, while others suggest a high-carbohydrate, low-protein diet is the key to health. Both argue the other is bad for you. I've tried both. You probably have as well.

Radio, television, books, and magazines are littered with experts dispensing advice. For years, they told us to eat whole grains. Now, we are being told the gluten in wheat is making us sick. The Gluten-Free Diet is certainly gaining in popularity. I tried it years ago when there weren't many options, and the food tasted like cardboard, or at least what I imagine cardboard would taste like if I were to eat it. Some of the gluten-free foods are actually pretty good now and most restaurants have a gluten-free menu. But generally, people don't stick with it even if it does help them feel better. I heard one expert recently say you should avoid gluten-free diets because you won't get enough nutrients. Which is true? Or are they both wrong?

Voices all around you are giving contradictory advice. "Coffee is bad for you." "No! Coffee prevents cancer and heart disease and is good for the liver." "Avoid eggs at all cost." "Sorry! New studies show that eggs are actually good for you." "Eat this and don't eat that." "Wait a minute! We were wrong. Forget what we told you before. You should eat that food. It is good for you after all."

Enough already! How are you supposed to know what to do? Why doesn't the world—with all its expert "good" advice—just admit that they really don't know what they're talking about?

Fad diets are everywhere. Unscrupulous marketers are making a fortune on our gullibility. We're inundated with television and radio ads hyping the newest "revolutionary" idea with outrageous claims of success. Have you noticed most of these ads run in January and February after we've gained a few pounds at Christmas and made our New Year's resolutions? The ads quit running around March because the diets don't work, and most people have abandoned their New Year's resolutions by then. Did you know that ninety-five percent of all diets fail, and most people eventually end up weighing more shortly after they quit a diet than when they started it? We Americans spend more than 60 billion (with a b) dollars every year on weight loss and weight-loss products. Seriously? We spend billions of dollars on something with a ninety-five percent failure rate!

And the latest crazes are getting crazier every year! Have you heard of the Cabbage Soup Diet? All you have to do is eat cabbage soup several times a day and restrict all other calories and you'll lose ten pounds in seven days! Of course, you will! If you eat only soup every day, you will lose weight. You don't have to go to medical school to figure that out. But how long are you going to keep it up? Even the creator of the Cabbage Soup Diet issues the disclaimer that you should not be on the diet for longer than seven days.

So, then what is the point? You lose ten pounds in seven days only to gain it all back when you start eating real foods, and after you go off the diet, you go right back to your starting weight. Not only that, but your body is mad at you for making it eat cabbage soup for seven days! It thinks you were starving to death and there must be a famine in the land. When you start eating again, your body thinks it needs to store as much fat as possible, and within a few days, you weigh more than when you started the diet. You're worse off than if you had never tried it. The website for the diet even states the following: "The Cabbage Soup Diet is not suitable for long-term weight loss." No kidding! No one is going to follow that diet for very long.

If cabbage soup doesn't tickle your taste buds, there is always the Cotton Ball Diet. Weight loss turns out to be much easier than anyone ever thought. All you need to do is dip five cotton balls in orange juice and eat them before every meal. Supposedly, the cotton balls settle in your stomach and make you feel full faster. I can see how that would work. If I ate five cotton balls, even if they were dipped in chocolate, I doubt I would have much of an appetite! Before you run off and buy a gallon of orange juice and a bag of cotton balls, you might want to know that cotton balls are not easily digestible and can create blockages in your intestines, meaning, you might need surgery to have the cotton balls removed. If they become infected, surgeons might have to remove part of your colon. Other than that, it's a great diet! Having part of your colon removed is certainly one way to lose weight.

There's the Baby Food Diet. I read that Jennifer Aniston, Lady Gaga, and Reese Witherspoon have all tried this diet. I don't know about you, but I'm not going to take eating advice from Lady Gaga. You eat fourteen jars of baby food every day. Seriously? I can't see myself going to a business meeting, and when my associates order steak, lobster, or fish, I pull out baby food! I think I'll bring baby food to the next church pot-luck dinner and see how that goes over. Let's see how many people choose baby food over pies, cakes, and mashed potatoes. I don't remember that far back, but I doubt I wanted to eat baby food even when I was a baby. I like solid foods. I think that's why God gave us teeth. The only reason babies eat baby food is that their parents force it down their throats. Someone would have to force fourteen jars of baby food a day down my throat right after they waterboarded me. They should call it the Torture Diet!

There is the Vision Diet. You wear blue-tinted glasses at every meal. The blue tint is supposed to make the food look less appetizing, so you eat less. I don't think it's very popular. I can't recall ever seeing anyone at a Mexican restaurant wearing blue tinted glasses. Again, I don't see myself pulling out blue-tinted glasses at a business meeting or a church picnic. Along the same lines, there's the Clothespin Diet. You clip a clothespin to your nose to block the smell of the food, and then you'll eat less. I haven't seen anyone at McDonald's with a clothespin on their nose either. I think I'll pull out a clothespin at homegroup next week. I would love to see the reaction when I tell everyone it is my new diet plan!

There's the Ice Cream Cleanse. You only eat ice cream every day. Now you're talking! That's certainly better than the Cotton Ball and the Cabbage Soup Diets. If you're only going to eat one thing every day, make it ice cream. For me, I'd probably prefer the Chocolate Pie Diet or the Macaroni and Cheese Diet. Honestly, I love chocolate pie and mac and cheese, but I don't want to eat either of them every day no matter how much I love them.

The weirdest one I read about was the Tapeworm Diet. I hope you aren't squeamish. In this diet, you take a pill that has a live tapeworm egg inside it. When the egg hatches, it settles in your stomach and intestines and eats everything you eat—that prevents the calories from getting into your bloodstream. It prevents the nutrients from getting into your body as well, but that's the least of your worries. The reported side effects are diarrhea, pain in the abdomen, nausea, feelings of weakness, fever, neurological issues, vision problems, organ failure, blockages of ducts, liver failure, and eventually death. You'll lose weight though, especially after you die!

You can't make these things up.

I think the word diet should be classified as a dirty, four-letter word and we should all be forbidden to speak it. Our mouths should be washed out with soap every time we say the word. That could be a new diet: The Soap Diet. Every time you have a craving to eat something, you wash your mouth out with soap. I imagine the soap taste would curb your appetite. If it did, you'd lose weight. I may be on to something. The Soap Diet could make me millions! That'll be my next book.

Fad diets aren't going to go away. Entrepreneurs will keep coming up with advertising gimmicks to play on people's emotions and get them to waste their money on their newest schemes. We're impulsive and impatient people looking for a quick fix to a serious problem. We're willing to try even the dumbest things, like the Grapefruit Diet. In this diet, you eat grapefruit every day while restricting your calories to a thousand a day. It doesn't take a genius to conclude that if you only eat grapefruit every day and little else, you will lose weight.

That is why these plans are so misleading. Read the fine print. Most of them say they should be used in conjunction with a low-calorie diet and exercise plan. You can eat chocolate cake every day, and if you restrict your total calories to a thousand a day, you will undoubtedly lose weight! But you'll gain it back and then some when you quit the diet, which you inevitably will. There's no way you can stay on these plans for the rest of your life. Did God really intend for you to eat just grapefruits? When He created cotton, did He really intend it to be used for food?

These diets would be funny if they weren't such a serious problem. People are really hurting and suffering because of their desperate need to lose weight. I realize the anxiety, depression, and social pressure to be healthy scares people and drives them to try almost anything that will help them lose weight. That's the reason I wrote this book. It's not to make fun of diets or people who go on them but rather to show you there is a better and more effective way to lose weight. It has been right there in the Bible all along; we've just never really seen it. I'll share more on this later.

The word diet is not really a bad word. Webster's Dictionary defines it as food and drink that is regularly consumed. The word diet comes from the Latin word "diaeta" and the Greek word "diaita," which literally mean way of living. That's the best way to look at a diet. It's healthiest when it's considered a way of living.

Webster's has a second meaning for the word, which is "a regimen of eating and drinking sparingly for weight loss." That's a more common and familiar definition and a more modern phenomenon. However, the true definition of diet is not about restricted eating. I want you to take that second meaning out of your vocabulary. After reading this book, you'll never go on a "diet" again. This book is based on the first meaning, not the second. It's called *The Jesus Diet* because it's based on a way of living modeled by Jesus, reaffirmed and taught by Paul in the epistles through revelations he received from Jesus.

The Jesus Diet is going to transform what you think about food, drink, diet, weight loss, and health once and for all. I'm so glad you picked up this book and are reading it. When you first saw the title, you might have thought it was another fad diet or unique angle to dieting. That's okay. Even if you were searching for another angle or gimmick diet, at least you're interested in knowing what Jesus said about the topic.

I guarantee you that the Jesus Diet is not a fad diet. You may be worried that the Jesus Diet requires eating locusts and wild honey like John the Baptist did. You may think it's like the Daniel fast and severely restricts meat and any food that "tastes good." You may think it's based on the Mediterranean Diet since that is generally what Jesus ate. There's nothing necessarily wrong with any of those diets, but this book is nothing like them. In fact, it's not a diet at all but a way of living. That's why the word diet is marked through in the title. It's based on a few simple principles Jesus taught that we have mostly overlooked and are a diet only in the sense of it's our way of eating.

Most diet books tell you what you can and can't eat. Most suggest meal plans and even recipes. You won't find anything like that in this book. A friend of mine asked me at church last Sunday if the Jesus Diet means that he can't eat meat and that if it did, he wasn't going to read it! I told him it's nothing like that at all. Let me reassure you. You'll be amazed at what you can eat on the Jesus Diet.

The Jesus Diet has transformed my life. Once I began implementing its principles, I immediately saw a change in my overall health. My wife has studied health and wellness for more than ten years. She was skeptical when I first started talking to her about the Jesus Diet. She wasn't sure it would work. She proofread every chapter I wrote, and by Chapter Five, she was convinced that it works. She said she couldn't believe we had never seen this before. She started implementing the principles of my book and has experienced the same improvements in her health that I have.

It works. I believe that the Jesus Diet will be a tremendous success. It will not have a ninety-five percent failure rate like the other diets. I believe that the Jesus Diet is going to transform how the body of Christ approaches diets, food, and wellness.

Here are our goals:

1. To help you permanently get off the "yoyo" diet cycle that is based on legalism and the law that Jesus set us free from in the new covenant of grace.
2. To get out of the world's system of diet and exercise as the means to good health and into God's system of divine health.
3. To learn how and why you can eat foods that are bad for you without being harmed by them.
4. To free yourself from the guilt, shame, and condemnation that you have struggled with for years because of your inability to change your health by your own efforts.

5. To learn to be thankful for food, not to fear it.

6. To learn to enjoy food in the way God intended.

7. To learn the true meaning of the Lord's Supper.

Above all else, you are going to experience and live out the abundant life that Jesus promised you by following His diet plan (way of living plan) for your life. It's so simple that you are going to wonder why you never heard of it before now.

CHAPTER 2
THE HISTORY OF FOOD LAWS AND EATING DISORDERS

The power of sin is the law. (1 Corinthians 15: 56 NIV)

People have a love–hate relationship with food. We love to eat but hate the ongoing struggle that food can create. For centuries, governments and religions have placed laws and restrictions on food and drink. Many of them are completely unexplainable.

For instance, in Alabama, there's a law making it illegal to carry an ice cream cone in your back pocket. While putting an ice cream cone in your pocket seems like a bad idea, why is it a law? If the government hadn't made that law, my wife, who does my laundry, would have. Still, it seems unnecessary. My wife has never had to tell me not to put an ice cream cone in my pants. I wouldn't even think to do that, and I can't see any good reason why anyone else would either. I thought this law must be unique to one city in Alabama, but then I learned there are similar laws in Kentucky and Georgia. Apparently, pocket ice cream cones are a bigger problem than I realized.

In Greene, New York, it's against the law to eat peanuts and walk backward. I tried to give lawmakers the benefit of the doubt and assumed there must be a good reason for the law, but then I learned the same thing is illegal in Ridley Park, Pennsylvania. Apparently, eating peanuts and walking backward is a real problem in Pennsylvania and New York. Is walking backward while eating an East Coast thing? Apparently not. It's illegal in Marion, Ohio, to eat a donut and walk backward. Why just peanuts and donuts? Are those the only foods people eat walking backward? I haven't tried it, but I doubt I could chew gum and walk backward, much less eat a meal!

It is illegal to buy alcohol in stores on Sundays in some counties in Arkansas. There are probably some religious reasons behind the ban, but why do some of those counties still allow it to be served in restaurants on Sunday? In Ohio, it's against the law to eat Corn Flakes on Sunday. In St. Cloud, Minnesota, it's illegal to eat hamburgers on Sunday. Come on! Someone please explain to me how prohibiting Corn Flakes and hamburgers keeps the Sabbath day holy.

In Oklahoma, however, it is illegal to take a bite out of another person's hamburger any day of the week! I need to remember that when we travel there. My wife takes a bite out of my hamburgers all the time! I didn't realize I was married to a lawbreaker and a repeat offender no less. My wife insists she has never taken a bite of my hamburger in Oklahoma, but I'm not so sure, at least not to where I could testify in a court of law. Is there a statute of limitations for that offense? We haven't been to Oklahoma in a few years, so I think she's in the clear.

In Massachusetts, it is against the law to eat more than three sandwiches at a funeral wake. I don't know why. At my funeral, everyone can eat all the sandwiches they want. They can have an open sandwich bar for all I care. I won't be there. In Maryland, it's against the law to eat while swimming in the ocean. That makes some sense. Food in the water could be bad for ocean wildlife and might pollute the water. In a city in South Carolina, it's against the law to eat watermelon in a cemetery. I'm dying to know why (pun intended)!

Okay. These are public places, and the local governments should be able to create their own laws. If they don't legislate what we do in the privacy of our own homes, I don't have a problem with it. But not so fast. In California, it's against the law to eat an orange in your bathtub! How do they enforce that law? Do they have a special division of the police force inspecting bathtubs for evidence of orange consumption? Is there a forensic test for orange peel residue? Interestingly, it's also against the law to keep a horse in a bathtub. What would happen if you fed a horse an orange in the bathtub? Could they put you away for years?

For centuries, religions all over the world have imposed religious laws on what and how people eat. In one religion, it is forbidden to eat with your left hand. I'm right-handed so it wouldn't affect me, but it seems discriminatory against left-handed people. Another religion forbids the consumption of cows because they are considered gods and goddesses and need to be protected. I don't get it. My parents used to own cows, and I have seen them up close. They are not gods. I know there is only one God, and He is not a cow. He created cows, but not in His image.

One religion forbids eating animals of any kind. Their belief is that eating an animal allows its spirit to come inside you, along with the nature of the animal when it was killed. In other words, eating animals causes a person to be tormented with the same suffering the animal endured when it was slaughtered for food. Their way of thinking is called karma.

Meats are not the only foods prohibited by some religions. One forbids potatoes, onions, garlic, and any underground vegetable. Adherents are also forbidden from eating honey and can only drink unfiltered water. Food can only be eaten during daylight hours. No midnight snacks are allowed. A late-night run to McDonald's for French fries would break two laws!

Why are humans so obsessed with the regulation of food with rules and laws? It is human nature to love food, but we make it bad in some way by creating laws and regulations. Humans have developed a distorted and almost perverse relationship with food that has persisted through the ages. We must go back to the beginning of time to understand when it started and why.

Food as nourishment for the body was God's idea. In the beginning, God created herbs and trees that yielded seeds and said, "To you it shall be for food" (Genesis 1:29). He placed man in the Garden of Eden and made "every tree grow that is pleasant to the sight and good for food" (Genesis 2:9). God intended food to be something good for us. He looked at everything He created and said that it was "very good" (Genesis 1:31).

God made a rule about food in the Garden of Eden. Adam and Eve could eat the fruit from any tree in the garden except the tree of knowledge of good and evil. He warned them, "For in the day that you eat of it you shall surely die" (Genesis 2:16–17). Not only did God create a rule associated with food, but there was punishment as well. Eat the wrong food, and you will die!

You know the story of how Adam and Eve ate the fruit and sin and death entered the world. Because of their actions, they were cast out of the garden and were cursed, and an association between food and punishment was established. Instead of food being good for man, it became the reason why man was cursed. Man realized that the improper use of food could result in bad behavior that would make God mad.

The first murder occurred over food. Cain killed his brother Abel because God accepted Abel's food sacrifice but not his (Genesis 4:8). Abel lost his life, and Cain was severely punished because of food. From the very beginning, food, bad behavior, and punishment were interconnected and became embedded in man's nature.

Years later, God brought the children of Israel out of Egypt and gave them a new set of laws to follow. The Levitical law also known as Mosaic law. These laws were the basis for the old covenant. They were given to Moses and were detailed instructions on how to live. Of the 613 laws, twenty-eight were dietary, with instructions on what and what not to eat.

In the dietary laws, God defined foods as either clean or unclean. Clean foods were good to eat; unclean foods were forbidden. Do you see the pattern? God categorized food in the garden as good fruit and forbidden fruit, and He categorized food under the law as clean and unclean. Same concept, just different terminology. You can find a list of those foods in Leviticus 11 and Deuteronomy 14. You should read them if you haven't already. It is fascinating to read what God wanted the children of Israel to eat.

I believe God gave them the dietary laws based on what was good for them. He wasn't establishing laws just for the sake of having laws. He wasn't creating a vehicle by which to punish them. He created their bodies and knew what foods were best for them. He was simply giving them instructions on which foods were healthy and which foods were unhealthy. Clean foods were good for their bodies; unclean foods were bad. You can learn a lot about health by studying God's dietary laws.

Punishment was attached to not following the law. Everyone knew the laws and was expected to follow them to the letter or face the consequences. It became ingrained in their culture. They lived under the Mosaic law for more than 1500 years before Christ came. God considered the keeping of the dietary laws a matter of holiness. He said in Leviticus 11:44–47:

> For I am the Lord your God. You shall therefore consecrate yourselves, and you shall be holy; for I am holy. Neither shall you defile yourselves with any creeping thing that creeps on the earth. For I am the Lord who brings you up out of the land of Egypt, to be your God. You shall therefore be holy, for I am holy.

> This is the law of the animals and the birds and every living creature that moves in the waters, and of every creature that creeps on the earth, to distinguish between the unclean and the clean, and between the animal that may be eaten and the animal that may not be eaten.

Remember verse forty-four, especially the part about consecrating yourself. It's going to be important to your understanding of the Jesus Diet in future chapters. God considered eating clean foods a matter of holiness. When they ate foods that were clean, they were consecrating themselves and were holy. When they ate foods that were unclean, they defiled themselves. That was considered an abomination. The definition of abomination is something that causes disgust or hatred. God hated it and was disgusted when man violated His dietary laws and ate something unclean.

Adam and Eve were not really under any pressure to keep the law in the Garden until Satan began to tempt them. The children of Israel, however, were under constant pressure to keep the dietary laws. That is a consequence of sin entering the world. Man had a clear choice between good and evil. In Deuteronomy 30:19, God said:

> I call heaven and earth as witnesses today against you, that I have set before you life and death, blessing and cursing; therefore, choose life, that both you and your descendants may live.

It was literally a matter of life and death. Choosing to eat clean foods produced life and a blessing. Choosing to eat unclean foods was essentially choosing a curse and death. They knew that something bad would happen if they broke the laws. They also knew the rewards if they kept them:

> And the Lord will take away from you all sickness, and will afflict you with none of the terrible diseases of Egypt,, which you have known, but will lay them on all those who hate you. (Deuteronomy 7:15)

Divine health came through keeping the laws. The children of Israel were promised a life free from sickness and disease if they ate only clean foods, because clean foods were consecrated and would not hurt their bodies. Remember that concept for later.

Keeping this law was easier said than done. They could not follow the law perfectly and were under constant threat of punishment. Why couldn't they keep the law, knowing it would be good for them and they would be rewarded with divine health?

The Bible says man has a sinful nature. Romans 5:12 says sin entered the world through Adam's sin in the garden. Psalm 51:5 says man was born into iniquity. All subsequent generations were born into sin. Man often finds it difficult to avoid doing what is bad for him, but it's not his fault. He inherited this from Adam. The children of Israel could not keep the laws of clean and unclean foods because it was in their nature to do the wrong thing.

They also inherited from Adam a cycle of behavior related to food. For Adam, food was categorized as being good to eat or bad to eat. Eat what was bad, and you would be punished. Adam was tempted, ate the wrong food, felt guilt, shame, and condemnation, and suffered devastating consequences.

The children of Israel experienced the exact same thing. Foods were categorized as clean or unclean. They were tempted to eat the wrong foods, ate them, felt guilt, shame, and condemnation, and then they were punished. That cycle came from Adam, and it has been passed on to every subsequent generation like it is firmly rooted in our DNA.

Fast forward to Jesus's day. As if keeping Mosaic law wasn't hard enough, the Pharisees added to it with their traditions. Jesus called them "human rules":

So, the Pharisees and teachers of the law asked Jesus, "Why don't your disciples live according to the tradition of the elders instead of eating their food with defiled hands?"

He replied, "Isaiah was right when he prophesied about you hypocrites; as it is written:

"These people honor me with their lips, but their hearts are far from me.

They worship me in vain; their teachings are merely **human rules**.

You have let go of the commands of God and are holding on to human traditions." (Mark 7: 5–8 NIV) (Emphasis Added)

The Pharisees and teachers of the law were the regulatory agencies of Jesus's day. They took upon themselves the responsibility to interpret the Mosaic law given by God. The problem was they not only interpreted the laws but added their own rules and regulations. Those were the "traditions of the elders." Remember, they had 1500 years to keep adding to the Mosaic law. So many traditions were added to the law that, after many years, it was hard to distinguish between what was law and what was tradition. The Pharisees basically made no distinction. They required everyone to follow both. Jesus kept the law but rejected their traditions. He said they were actually "letting go of the commands of God" to hold on to their own human traditions.

They confronted Jesus because His disciples weren't keeping the human rule and were eating with what the Pharisees called "defiled" hands (v.5). Jesus said His disciples didn't have to keep them. Those so-called laws were vain teachings. He even called their worship vain. They thought they were following those traditions to please God when they were hypocrites feeling good about themselves for doing something God had never told them to do. It was all in vain. They were not scoring any points with God. They were adding to the law and placing more restrictions on the people. Jesus refused to comply. Jesus kept the Mosaic law perfectly, but He wasn't about to keep any laws created by man, only those laws commanded by God.

Man has been creating his own laws ever since. I mentioned a few of the ridiculous ones at the beginning of this chapter. We create laws and traditions that have nothing to do with what God has commanded us to do. "Human rules," while often well-meaning, create burdens and unreasonable expectations that are impossible to meet. In America, we are obsessed with making laws.

At the time of this writing, the United States tax code consists of 2,652 pages of laws. At an average of 450 words per page, the code is more than one million words. That doesn't include the regulations in the code. Add all the regulations and there are more than nine thousand pages and more than four million words!

A few years ago, Congress passed a new health care law called the Affordable Care Act, generally known as Obamacare. There are 2,700 pages in the new law. There are three pages of regulations for every page of law. That adds up to a total of 10,535 pages of laws and regulations, or 11,508,500 words. There are only 788,280 words in the entire Bible!

When it comes to food and drink, there are two departments in the federal government: The Food and Drug Administration (FDA) and the United States Department of Agriculture (USDA). The FDA regulates everything related to food and drink along with drugs and supplements. It has more than fifteen thousand employees, and more than three thousand state and local agencies. The USDA regulates and inspects the production of food and has more than one hundred thousand employees and thirty-three agencies. There are millions of laws on the books related to food and drink. Several futile attempts have been made to count the total number of laws in the United States legal code. There are too many to count. The number of laws and regulations regarding food and drink are impossible to count or comprehend. God only needed twenty-eight!

It is in man's nature to legislate food. That is where these regulations and food laws come from. Sometimes, he does it through silly laws and regulations. Sometimes, it's through legalistic religious structure. Today, it's also through regulating our food with diets. A "diet" is nothing more than a self-imposed law that restricts something you want to eat.

You categorize foods as clean and unclean by creating your own set of diet rules. You don't use those terms, but it's reflected in the words you speak: "I can't eat that. That's not on my diet. I have to avoid those foods." You identify and classify clean foods as those you can eat on your diet. Every diet is different, but they are all based on a set of rules and regulations that restrict what you can and can't eat. Most diets restrict the number of calories. Some even make you count the calories. Others assign points to food and give you a daily allowance of points. Some diets regulate the time of day you can eat, while others regulate the number of meals you can eat each day. Some restrict carbs; others restrict proteins. Some restrict breads; others restrict portion sizes. The common denominator is that they all establish a set of rules that you must follow. It's difficult to think about food without categorizing them as either good or bad for you.

The problem comes when your sinful nature kicks in and you classify the inability to keep "human rules" as bad behavior. When you eat something that's not on your diet, you say you ate something bad. Does this sound familiar? "I was bad. I ate that dessert." "I'm going to cheat on my diet and have that piece of cake." When you have the willpower to pass on food, you say, "I was good." "Are you proud of me? I didn't have that dessert." You attach rewards to food. "If I'm good this week, I can have birthday cake this weekend." You attach punishment to the diet. When you don't keep the rules and regulations perfectly, which you never will, then you feel like a failure.

A diet is nothing more than a modern-day re-creation of the Old Testament dietary laws. They are your laws, not God's. They are human rules, not the commands of God. It is your way of regulating your food through self-effort. The old covenant is based on self-effort. That's why it failed. Man could not keep the law perfectly. You can't keep the diet perfectly either. God doesn't punish you any more for eating the wrong foods, so you punish yourself.

That behavior is an eating disorder. Not in the clinical sense, but an eating disorder is defined as a disturbed or abnormal eating pattern. A diet is nothing more than an abnormal eating pattern that disturbs your normal routine of eating. A disorder is defined as a state of confusion. You're in a state of confusion as to what you should eat. That's why most people jump from diet to diet. You are confused. You know you need to do something; you're just not sure what. And the world is not helping matters with its conflicting advice and gimmick diets. Others take what's in your nature and profit from it.

There is a theory in psychology called psychological behaviorism. It holds that behaviors are learned, most during our formative years. You are programmed at an early age to respond to circumstances in a certain way based on what you experience. As an adult, you often react to circumstances based on the behaviors you learned as a child. Negative childhood experiences create negative behaviors as an adult. That is why sexual and physical abuse are so destructive for children. Disorders, addictions, anxiety, depression, fears, and all manner of emotional problems can often be linked to severe trauma or abuse as a child and can become learned negative behaviors for an adult.

It doesn't have to always be negative. Positive experiences as a child create positive responses later in life. Pavlov famously developed an experiment where a dog was rewarded with food when he heard a ringing bell. The classical conditioning response was, after hearing the bell repeatedly, the dog eventually responded to the bell, seeking food. The dog developed an unconditional response to the bell and even salivated every time he heard it. That's like when you drive by Krispy Kreme donuts and see the "Hot Donuts" sign. You begin salivating. That is an unconditioned response and is psychological behaviorism.

It's in your nature to regulate food, but it's also a learned behavior from childhood. You were taught as a child to associate food with punishment. "Eat your vegetables, and you can have dessert. Don't eat your vegetables, and you'll go to bed with no dessert." "If you clean your room, you can have ice cream. If you don't, you'll be punished and will go to bed with no supper." That is psychological behaviorism. It is also placing your kids under the law.

The problem is you can't keep the diets any more than Adam and Eve or the children of Israel could follow God's instructions. You live out the same cycle they lived out. You categorize food as either good or bad. You're tempted to eat the bad food, and then you feel guilt, shame, and condemnation for your failures. These negative emotions are your way of punishing yourself for eating the wrong foods.

I was at church recently and overheard a member talking about her new diet. She has eliminated all carbs. She was describing how hard it was not to eat bread. She said that she has been "cheating" some. Those were her words. She said that she loved breaded foods. She would take off half of the breading on a piece of okra and only eat half of each piece with breading on it. She sounded defensive and guilty for eating the half-breaded food. That's exactly what I am talking about. She has created her own law that she cannot perfectly follow. She'll eventually give up. When she does, she'll feel like a failure.

There is a better way. The Jesus Diet is the better way. I hesitate to call it a diet based on what I just wrote about diets. Remember the definition of diet in Chapter One. The Jesus Diet is a way of living. You will see it has nothing to do with the law or diets defined as the restriction of food. The Jesus Diet is a way of living that will transform how you see food forever. You just don't know what it is yet. The first step is understanding why you do what you do when it comes to food. Your next step is to resist the sinful nature within you that wants to regulate food and to reject the learned behavior associating food with punishment you were taught as a child.

Jesus said He is the way, truth, and the life (John 14:6) and He is the way of living when it comes to diet, food, and divine health. He lived under the dietary laws of the old covenant given to Moses by God. He followed those laws perfectly, never eating anything considered unclean. How do we know that? He was without sin, and eating unclean foods was a sin and an abomination to the Lord (1 Peter 2:22, 2 Corinthians 5:21). Jesus would have never done anything that was an abomination to the Lord.

Does that mean that the Jesus Diet is eating what Jesus ate? Does that mean that we are to keep the old covenant dietary laws just like Jesus did? No! The Jesus Diet is based on what Jesus taught, not necessarily about what he ate or what laws He followed. In the next chapter, you are going to learn the first principle of the Jesus Diet: Jesus changed everything as it relates to food.

CHAPTER 3
YOU ARE WHAT YOU EAT ARE FREE TO EAT

For the law was given through Moses,
but grace and truth came through Jesus Christ. (John 1:17)

A greeting card said the following:

> Dear Diet, Things are just not going to work out between us. I
> am breaking up with you. It's not me. It's you. You are tasteless,
> boring, and I can't stop cheating on you.

Break up with your diet. Throw diet books away that contain "human rules." Resist the temptation to go into the bondage of a diet. Your sinful nature will keep drawing you back to the law. The world will keep hyping diets, trying to get you back into bondage to food by categorizing foods as good or bad. Why would the Bible say that Jesus set you free from the law of sin and death if you weren't in bondage to it? The enemy would like nothing more than to keep you under a set of rules and regulations and the cycle of sin and death.

By the end of this chapter, you are going to be set free! You may not realize that you need to be set free, but you do. When it comes to food and drink, we all do. John 8:32 says, "You shall know the truth, and the truth shall make you free." You are about to learn the truth about food and drink once and for all, and the truth will set you free. You are about to be set free from bondage to food and drink. You are about to be set free from the law.

Paul said in Romans that we are no longer under the law but under grace:

> For sin shall not have dominion over you, for you are not under law but under grace. (Romans 6:14)

> Because through Christ Jesus the law of the Spirit who gives life has set you free from the law of sin and death. (Romans 8:2 NIV)

When Jesus came to this earth, everything changed. Man was no longer under the law, but under grace and truth (John 1:17). Paul was referring to the Mosaic law in the above verse in Romans. Not that you ever even had the opportunity to be under the law of Moses. The law was between the children of Israel and God. It never applied to you. You were born after Christ died. Any attempts you make to put yourself under the law are in vain. Not that you would ever want to be under the law of the old covenant. It required strict obedience, or punishment was the result. Paul was under the law for much of his life, so he knew firsthand the bondage it created.

Christ established a new covenant of grace through His death on the cross. Why a new covenant? Because man could not keep the first covenant. The new covenant is better. It was established on better promises:

> But now He has obtained a more excellent ministry, inasmuch as He is also Mediator of a better covenant, which was established on better promises. For if that first covenant had been faultless, then no place would have been sought for a second. (Hebrews 8:6–7)

You should be thankful that you are not under the old covenant laws. They were too hard to keep. Under the law, man did the work. Under grace, Jesus did the work on our behalf. Under the law, God demanded strict obedience to produce righteousness. Under grace,

Jesus provided righteousness as a gift. Under the law, there was no negotiation. Follow the law or else. Under grace, Jesus negotiated a better covenant as our mediator. The new covenant is between Jesus and God. We are just the benefactors. You get the benefits by believing in Jesus.

What a great deal Jesus mediated on your behalf. That sounds too good to be true, so most people don't take advantage of the blessings. Part of the better deal is that you no longer must follow any of the dietary laws. If you no longer have to follow the dietary laws of the old covenant, then what are the dietary instructions under the new covenant? Jesus addressed that in Mark 7: 14–19 NIV:

> Again Jesus called the crowd to him and said, "Listen to me, everyone, and understand this. Nothing outside a person can defile them by going into them. Rather, it is what comes out of a person that defiles them."

> After he had left the crowd and entered the house, his disciples asked him about this parable. "Are you so dull?" he asked. "Don't you see that nothing that enters a person from the outside can defile them? For it doesn't go into their heart but into their stomach, and then out of the body." (In saying this, Jesus declared all foods clean).

JESUS DIET PRINCIPLE #1
Jesus made all foods clean.

Jesus declared all foods clean. He said nothing that enters a person from the outside can defile them. Nothing. No food you eat can defile you. No drink you consume can defile you. There are no dietary instructions under the new covenant other than that all foods are available for you to eat. With that one statement, Jesus totally changed the law of clean and unclean and fifteen hundred years of rules, regulations, and traditions that governed what people ate. Under the new covenant, nothing you eat is sinful anymore.

Under the Jesus Diet, no foods and no drinks are prohibited. No law you place on food is applicable. Jesus did not place any restrictions on food, and you shouldn't either. Therefore, every so-called "diet" that prohibits and restricts food and drink is contrary to Jesus's instruction. In this one statement, Jesus set you free forever from any restrictions related to food and drink, and He eliminated any need for "diets." In fact, the "diet" becomes the sin because it is your vain attempt to change your health by your own works.

That requires a total shift in your thinking. It's a matter of believing what Jesus said is true. If you believe Jesus made all foods clean, you'll never go on a diet again. A diet says there are certain foods you can't eat. Jesus said you can eat anything.

My wife was with a friend who knows I am writing this book and asked how it was coming. Several friends who were nearby overheard the conversation, and one asked Donna, "What is the name of the book?"

She replied, "It is called The Jesus Diet."

The lady said, "How interesting! What foods are restricted in the Jesus Diet?"

Donna said no foods are restricted.

The lady retorted, "Then it's not really a diet. You should take the word diet out of the title."

No! A diet is a way of living, not a restriction of food. I reject any attempt by man to tell me I can't eat something. We need a complete paradigm shift to fully grasp this concept. Don't worry if you don't get it at first. Peter had a problem accepting this new covenant truth. Read Acts 10: 9–15 in the NIV:

About noon the following day as they were on their journey and approaching the city, Peter went up on the roof to pray. He became hungry and wanted something to eat, and while the meal was being prepared, he fell into a trance. He saw heaven opened and something like a large sheet being let down to earth by its four corners. It contained all kinds of four-footed animals, as well as reptiles and birds. Then a voice told him, "Get up, Peter. Kill and eat."

"Surely not, Lord!" Peter replied. "I have never eaten anything impure or unclean."

The voice spoke to him a second time, "Do not call anything impure that God has made clean."

Peter lived his whole life under the Mosaic law. The dream challenged everything he had ever been taught. According to him, he had kept the law perfectly. He said, "I have never eaten anything impure or unclean." He had a lot more willpower than most of us do. But Peter was conflicted. In the dream, the voice told him to abandon his beliefs and religious practices and eat foods that were unclean. Who was talking to Peter? Verse fourteen tells us that the Lord (Jesus) was speaking. Remember, this was after His ascension. Jesus was no longer with Peter in person. Peter recognized the voice, and Jesus admonished him not to call anything unclean God has made clean.

This is an interesting passage because Jesus declared all foods clean in Mark 7:19 while He was still alive. Peter said he had never eaten anything unclean. He lived with Jesus for three years. Jesus and his disciples never ate anything unclean in those three years. If Jesus declared all foods clean, why didn't He and His disciples eat unclean foods? Because Jesus had not yet died. They were still under the old covenant law of clean and unclean foods. The Bible should really be understood in terms of the old covenant and the new covenant. The old covenant ended when Jesus died. After His death, the old covenant became obsolete and no longer applicable:

In that He says, "A new covenant," He has made the first obsolete. Now what is becoming obsolete and growing old is ready to vanish away. (Hebrews 8:13)

The concept of foods as clean or unclean or good and bad is obsolete. The word *obsolete* means out of date. The old covenant is out of date. If you have a two-year warranty on a television, when the warranty runs out, it's of no use anymore. The dietary laws have run out and are no use anymore.

Like Peter, you may struggle with changing your beliefs. Voices around you reinforce the behavior. Friends and family say things like, "Do you really need to eat that much?" "She is pretty on the inside." "She has struggled with her weight all of her life." "She was chubby even as a baby." "Did you lose weight? You look better." These statements reinforce the idea that something is wrong with you. Nothing is wrong with you. You live under the grace of the new covenant.

Your words even mirror theirs: "Do I look fat?" "Does this dress make me look fat?" "I'm trying to lose weight." "I have struggled with weight my entire life." "I didn't have a weight problem until I had kids." "I have a slow metabolism, and that makes it hard for me to lose weight." "My thyroid is messed up, and I can't seem to lose weight because of it." We come up with thousands of excuses to try and cover up the guilt.

We even make excuses for why we eat certain foods. "Fast food is cheaper. Healthy foods are expensive." "I don't have time to cook at home." "I have a sweet tooth."

You make these excuses because you feel like you're doing something wrong and you need to justify the behavior. You don't have to make excuses. No one has any right to judge you. Jesus gave you permission to eat anything.

I was on a diet for several years that classified foods into three categories: beneficial, neutral, and avoid. I was doing the exact opposite of what God said to do in the new covenant. God said to not call anything impure that God has made clean. I shouldn't classify any food as avoid God said I could have. Like Peter, I need to be careful what I say. I need to quit saying, "I can't eat that." "That food is an avoid for me." "I can't have carbs." "I can't eat red meat." "I'm a vegetarian. I don't eat meat." That's not any different from Peter saying, "I can't eat that, it's unclean. I would never eat anything unclean." Those words were in direct opposition to what Jesus said. Paul said in Colossians 2 that you should not let anyone tell you what you should or should not eat or drink. They have no right to say if it is right or wrong to eat certain food. He went on to say those were human rules that should be ignored.

> You have died with Christ, and he has set you free from the spiritual powers of this world. So why do you keep on following the rules of the world, such as, "Don't handle! Don't taste! Don't touch!"? Such rules are mere human teachings about things that deteriorate as we use them. These rules may seem wise because they require strong devotion, pious self-denial, and severe bodily discipline. But they provide no help in conquering a person's evil desires. (Colossians 2: 20–23 NLT)

You need to reject those voices. The Bible is very clear that you should not let anyone tell you what you should or should not eat or drink. No one has the right to say something is right or wrong for you to eat.

You can eat anything without guilt. Aren't you glad? That should make you ecstatic! How many foods are clean? All of them. All means all. All carbohydrates are clean. All meats are clean. You can eat pork. You can eat shrimp. You can eat pie. You can eat cake. You can eat breaded foods. If Jesus said all foods are clean, who are you to contradict Jesus? Jesus wants to set you free. Be free and eat anything you want.

JESUS DIET PRINCIPLE #2

You can eat anything you want.

If you can believe that, then you're well on your way to reaching your ideal weight and divine health. I know that is counterintuitive. How do you lose weight when you can eat anything you want? How do you get healthy if you can eat unhealthy foods? You don't fully understand it yet. That's okay. There are many more principles to the Jesus Diet you're going to learn in the coming chapters. You'll understand it better by the end of the book. In fact, you'll know a lot more after reading the next chapter. It's going to explain a lot.

However, these two principles, Jesus made all foods clean, and you can eat anything you want, are the foundational principles you must first know. You'll find once you determine that all foods are not off limits anymore, you can break the power food has over your life, and the desire for them will diminish.

I read the blog of a lady who struggled with food and weight her entire life. One day, she decided she was going to quit fighting it. She made what she called "peace with food." She decided she could eat anything she wanted anytime she wanted. No restrictions. What she found was that the cravings went away. She no longer had a desire for those foods. She only had the desire when she couldn't have them. She began to lose weight. Her struggle with food was over.

Paul said in Romans 7: 8–12 that it's the law that creates the temptation:

> But sin used this command to arouse all kinds of covetous desires within me! If there were no law, sin would not have that power. At one time I lived without understanding the law. But when I learned the command not to covet, for instance, the power of sin came to life, and I died. So I discovered that the law's commands, which were supposed to bring life, brought spiritual death instead. Sin took advantage of those commands and deceived me; it

used the commands to kill me. But still, the law itself is holy, and its commands are holy and right and good. (NLT)

That's how it works. If you're not on a "diet," then you can't be tempted to break the diet. If all foods are available to you to eat, the temptation to eat a particular food is removed. How can you be tempted to sin if it's not wrong? Once the temptation is removed from the equation, the desire for the food leaves as well.

Psychological reactance is a behavioral response to a perceived threat to a person's freedom. The effect is that the more a person is told he or she can't do something, the stronger the desire becomes to do it. Often, the person wouldn't even have the desire if not for the banning of the action.

Children have a high tendency to respond with reactance. Reverse psychology is a way of manipulating reactance in children. For instance, if you want a child to go out and play, you tell him he must stay inside. That creates in the child the desire to go outside. His freedom to go outside has been challenged, and that creates an emotional response to reestablish his freedom. The child's reactance is to want to do something he is not allowed to do. There are several interesting studies that observed children in a room full of toys. If a child is told he can play with all the toys in the room except one, the child gravitates to that one toy. If that toy is never mentioned, the child ignores it and doesn't want to play with it unless it's in the normal course of playing.

Paul said it this way:

> I do not understand what I do. For what I want to do I do not do, but what I hate I do. (Romans 7:15 NIV)

> But I see another law in my members, warring against the law of my mind and bringing me into captivity to the law of sin which is in my members. (Romans 7:23)

Paul called it a war against the law of his mind. Paul knew he was free from the Mosaic law. He now needed deliverance from the captivity of the law within his mind that kept drawing him into the cycle of law, temptation, guilt, condemnation, sin, and death.

Paul went on to say in Romans 7:24–25:

> Who will deliver me from this body of death? I thank God through Jesus Christ my Lord.

Jesus will deliver you from this nature that wants to live under the law and desires to do the opposite of what the law tells you to do.

You're under your own law that's waging war within your mind. That law will try to draw you back into bondage to food through the law. You're not what you eat. You are what you are free to eat. If you can win the war within your mind, you can be set free from the laws of food that bring defeat. Christ has already done all the work. You must allow Him to defeat the law of sin and death in your mind and let Him free you from it forever.

Once you're delivered from the law, the temptation goes away. If there is no restriction on what you eat or drink, over time, you are not tempted by it. You may think if you give yourself permission to eat anything you want you will be eating all day long. The opposite is true. Once you are free from the law, you no longer have a desire to sin by breaking the law. Christ didn't make all foods clean so you could eat all day and weigh five hundred pounds. We'll talk about gluttony later in the book. Jesus made all foods clean so you wouldn't be a slave to food, you wouldn't desire the food, and you wouldn't be unhealthy and unhappy. Like the lady in the blog, make peace with food. Make peace with the war within you.

Some suggestions on how to make peace with food:

1. Give yourself permission to eat anything you want. Jesus already gave you permission.

2. Don't think of food in terms of good and bad. Clean and unclean is no longer applicable today.

3. Take the power away from the food. Take back control. You decide what you eat and drink and when you eat and drink it.

4. Eat when you are hungry. Stop when you are full.

5. Let yourself enjoy what you eat.

6. Don't let anyone else tell you what you can and cannot eat. Don't let anyone tell you what you are eating is wrong.

7. Let God change your desires. Don't try to change yourself by willpower.

Finally, don't try to be perfect. Reject any feelings of condemnation. Read Romans 8:1–3 in the NIV:

> Therefore, there is now no condemnation for those who are in Christ Jesus, because through Christ Jesus the law of the Spirit who gives life has set you free from the law of sin and death. For what the law was powerless to do because it was weakened by the flesh, God did by sending his own Son in the likeness of sinful flesh to be a sin offering.

What the diet was powerless to do, God did for you by sending His own Son Jesus. I hope you keep reading. We are just getting started in understanding the Jesus Diet. The next chapter is going to help you realize how you can eat unhealthy foods without being harmed by them.

CHAPTER 4
THE PROOF IS IN THANKING GOD
FOR THE PUDDING

Everything is lawful, but not everything is beneficial.
(1 Corinthians 10:23 NET)

I hope Jesus has convinced you all things are lawful to eat. Even so, Paul said in 1 Corinthians that not all things are beneficial. I am sure you have already thought of that fact. Even though Jesus made all foods clean, common sense would tell you there are still foods that are not healthy to eat. For instance, in the dietary laws of the old covenant, God said not to eat an animal found dead:

Do not eat anything you find already dead. You may give it to the foreigner residing in any of your towns, and they may eat it, or you may sell it to any other foreigner. But you are a people holy to the Lord your God. (Deuteronomy 14:21 NIV)

Why would God give them that instruction? If the animal is dead, it either died from old age or disease. Either way, it would be a risk to eat it. Under the new covenant, that dietary law no longer applies. It is obsolete. That doesn't change the fact that if you find an animal dead along the side of the road, you probably shouldn't eat it. It either died from a disease or has tire marks on its back!

You are inundated with advice on what to eat. There are literally thousands of diet books with instructions on what and what not to eat. Based on the first two principles of the Jesus Diet, I reject any book that says you can't eat something. Jesus said we could eat anything. That doesn't mean knowledge is not useful. If someone writes about food, weight loss, health, and wellness, explaining why something is healthy or unhealthy, it may be helpful. I read as many books on health as I can. At the same time, I'm skeptical of the world's advice.

There is no shortage of self-professed experts telling us what foods are healthy and unhealthy. I am not convinced they always know what they are talking about. Remember when experts said eat margarine because it was better for you than butter? Now we know it isn't better for you. The health establishment owes us an apology. Every study shows they were wrong. My grandmother never believed them and always used butter. My parents did believe them and made the switch to margarine. Turns out my grandmother was right, and the experts were wrong. I grew up eating something that was, unknowingly, bad for me.

A 1920s advertisement for cigarettes claimed 20,769 physicians endorsed their product. Cigarette companies fought over the endorsements of physicians shamelessly using their credibility to make the gullible public believe cigarettes were not bad for you. One advertisement in that era touted, "More physicians smoke Camels than any other cigarettes." Believing the experts, my grandfather developed throat cancer from smoking. He did eat butter and not margarine, though, thanks to my grandmother. I seem to remember her getting on him for his smoking as well.

The point is you may not know what is beneficial for you until years later. There are three different categories of foods that are lawful but might not be beneficial for you to eat today. First are unclean foods made clean by Jesus but that are still unhealthy for you. Remember, God declared foods unclean because they were unhealthy. Just because Jesus made them clean doesn't change the fact that they can be harmful to your body. Second are modern-day foods readily available today but not available when God made His original list of unclean foods. If God made a new list today, (which He won't do), there are a lot of foods we regularly eat that would be on it. Third are so-called "healthy" foods contaminated with pesticides, hormones, genetic modification, deadly bacteria, etc. These are the most problematic because we are eating what the experts say we should eat.

There are more than five thousand deaths per year and 325,000 hospitalizations in the United States from tainted foods, many of which are, supposedly, "healthy" choices. In June 2018, at least five people died from an E. coli outbreak tied to romaine lettuce. One hundred and ninety-five people in thirty-five states were sickened in the outbreak according to the Center for Disease Control and Prevention. Eighty-nine people were hospitalized and twenty-six of them developed kidney failure. I thought salads were the best food of choice.

In Europe, a listeria outbreak linked to frozen vegetables infected forty-seven people, killing nine of them. An outbreak of cyclophorias in contaminated vegetables infected more than a hundred people in two states. No one died, but the average person suffered from diarrhea that lasted an average of fifty-seven days!

I grew up thinking if I ate my spinach, I would be strong like Popeye. In 2006, two hundred people were hospitalized for eating spinach. Thirty-one developed kidney failure, and at least three people died. In North Dakota, a couple held a dinner party for twelve people in their home, where they served a salad sprinkled with peas. Sounds like a healthy meal. All twelve people fell ill and died. The canned peas were contaminated with botulism. It is said they died a very painful death.

A 2015 outbreak of salmonella in cucumbers infected a total of nine hundred and seven people in forty states across the country. Over two hundred people were hospitalized, and four deaths were attributed to the outbreak. A total of 265 people in eight states were infected with a strain of Salmonella typhimurium linked to chicken salad. In South Africa, one hundred and eighty deaths were linked to listeria found in deli meats. More than a thousand people were infected. They say we should eat more fruits. In 2011, 146 people in the United States were sickened from eating cantaloupe and thirty people died.

You have probably heard the slogan, "Milk does a body good." We're encouraged to drink more milk. In 1985, over five thousand people became violently ill drinking milk tainted with salmonella and nine people died. In 2008, more than three hundred thousand people in China were sickened by milk when melamine was added to the water. Melamine has been linked to liver failure in humans and is banned as a food additive in the United States. In Japan, 13,389 people were infected by powdered milk found to be laced with arsenic. More than six hundred people died. Juice is supposed to be better for you than soda. In 1996, sixty people fell ill, and one person died from drinking apple juice.

My wife is always telling me onions are good for me and is always trying to get me to eat them. In 2003, a hepatitis A outbreak linked to green onions sickened 555 people and killed three. You are told to eat more whole grains. In Iraq, 650 people were infected with methylmercury poisoning from eating wheat, and all 650 of them died.

We're told to eat more chicken and less red meat. In 2002, fifty people were sickened, and eight died from listeria found in chicken. Did you know chickens have been genetically enhanced to increase their growth? In 1920, an average chicken weighed 2.2 pounds. Today, the average chicken weighs 5.7 pounds! Chickens have always been a clean food for man to eat. Would God really consider them clean today with the modifications?

We are told we don't drink enough water. Water was God's idea and seemingly the best beverage choice for health, but our water supply is not how God originally created it. It is filtered, and chemicals are added. God didn't make water with fluoride. That was added by the government to help us have stronger teeth. God didn't add chlorine to our water supply. Man did that to kill contaminants. I admit those actions have probably protected us from getting sick. There is still an average of eighteen contaminants in our water supply. The levels are said to be low enough that they won't hurt us. It's still not what God created for us to drink. Bottled water is supposed to be an alternative to tap water, but now we are learning the plastic leaches into the water, especially when it's in the sun and gets hot. I don't want to drink plastic. In 2015, fourteen different brands of bottled water were recalled for E. coli contamination!

I realize those statistics are a small percentage when compared to how many people eat those foods and drink water. Perhaps those foods are better choices than many of the alternatives. Most of the time, you can eat fruits and vegetables and drink tap water and not get sick immediately. That doesn't mean our food is not making us sick over the long run. You can smoke a cigarette today, and it won't have any effect on your current health. Smoke a pack a day for thirty years, and you will see how destructive it is. You can eat almost anything today, and it won't have any dramatic effect on you if you don't get food poisoning. Eat those foods for forty years, even whole foods, and you'll see the effect.

I have read numerous diet books that say to eat the foods God created for you to eat. How is that possible? Most of the foods we eat are not foods God created for us to eat. Even the food God created for you to eat is modified by man. The book of Genesis says God gave us animals to eat and that they are good for food. Today, eighty percent of all antibiotics are prescribed for livestock and not for humans. God didn't create animals with antibiotics in them. Would God still say they were good for food? I don't know. God gave us fruits and vegetables to eat and said they were good for food. There are more than thirty-four thousand pesticides used on fruits and vegetables today. Are they still good for food? In 1996, two percent of soybeans were genetically modified. Today, ninety percent of all soybeans are genetically modified. We have changed the genetics and have modified the foods from how God initially created them. How could we possibly think that we can create better food than God?

Even if we eat organic and home-grown vegetables, they are still not harvested in the way God intended. God commanded the children of Israel to let the "land rest" every seven years so that the soil would be replenished with vitamins and minerals. We don't let land rest today. The demand for food is so great, farmers are growing as much as they can every year. They can't afford to go a whole year without crops on their land. They replenish the soil themselves by adding their own fertilizers and chemicals to help enrich the soil.

Did you know that seventy percent of our food is processed? We are not even eating whole foods. I'm convinced there really is not a healthy choice for us. Some foods are healthier than others, but that doesn't mean they are going to produce divine health like the Bible says God wants for us.

Don't take this the wrong way. I'm not criticizing the food industry. I am sure our farmers and meat producers are trying their best to deliver quality food to our tables. The modifications have allowed them to mass produce foods and deliver them to the grocery store shelves at reasonable prices. McDonald's provides fast food at an affordable price. Its food has been relatively safe in the short run, but over the long run, it has contributed to the public health problems. We all know intuitively that McDonald's Big Mac and fries aren't the best choice for health. Children's Happy Meals are not ideal for children's wellness. But they are convenient and inexpensive. Recently, McDonald's came out with salads to provide healthier choices. They just had a recall on the salads. Hundreds of people were getting sick from the lettuce!

I've read arguments that our food is safer than it has ever been due to techniques like genetic modification. The modifications are supposed to make the food healthier. We're told the levels of hormones in meat and pesticides in vegetables are so low they can't hurt us. They are supposedly needed to keep the animals from getting sicknesses and diseases that could harm us. Processed foods lengthen shelf life and protect the food from rotting. It has certainly been an important innovation. But I read how packaging can leach into the food and cause cancer. Are our packaged food and drinks good for us over many years? Are we going to find out years from now that genetically modified foods are like margarine and are actually harming our health?

Remember, our food is being regulated by more than 133,000 employees. Here are some of the laws that have been implemented by the FDA:

The FDA regulates canned mushrooms. The regulations say there cannot be more than twenty maggots per one hundred grams of drained mushrooms. There cannot be more than five maggots that are two millimeters or longer per hundred grams. Broccoli can have up to sixty mites per hundred grams.

Apples cannot have a mold content greater than twelve percent. Canned peaches are only allowed three percent of "wormy or moldy" content.

Do you like peanut butter? I don't know how many peanut butter and jelly sandwiches I ate as a child, but it was a lot. There's a law that says there can be no more than one rodent hair per hundred grams. I wonder how many rodent hairs I have eaten in my lifetime!

Apparently, fruit flies like to lay eggs in tomato sauce. There can be no more than fifteen fruit fly larvae per hundred grams of sauce. By the way, maggots like tomato sauce as well. You will be comforted to know there cannot be more than one maggot per hundred grams of tomato sauce. I wonder if maggots have anyone regulating their food. Do maggots really know if our tomato sauce and mushrooms are safe for them to eat?

My dad loves fig newtons. The FDA allows thirteen insect heads per hundred grams of fig newton paste. My dad is eighty-six and going strong, so I guess insect heads are good for you after all.

Ever wondered why spices add so much taste to food. The FDA allows up to 325 insect fragments per ten grams of the spice thyme. Ground cinnamon can have four hundred insect fragments per fifty grams. Ground oregano can have up to three hundred insect fragments per ten grams. These spices are all ground. I wonder if the insect fragments are only fragments because they were ground. Maybe there were whole insects in the spices, and they were all ground together.

Apparently, rodent hairs like spices as well as peanut butter. The FDA allows nine rodent hairs per ten grams of spice. Paprika is allowed eleven rodent hairs. I have no idea why, but nutmeg is only allowed one. That may become my spice of choice.

Did you lose your appetite? That might be a good weight-loss plan. Anytime you are hungry, just reread this chapter, and you won't be hungry anymore!

I'm not making a political statement here. I'm glad the government regulates food, and I know it's impossible to keep food from having some contamination. I'm sure the men and women of these agencies are sincere and doing a great job. The point is, even if we make what we think are the right choices, how do we really know the foods are healthy? The proof is in the pudding, which, by the way, has a shelf life of ten years. Seriously! Can any food with that long a shelf life really be good for us?

What should we think about these statistics? In 1990, there were 12.5 million Americans with asthma. In 2000, there were twenty-five million Americans with asthma. The number doubled in ten years.

Kidney-related diseases have doubled in the last decade. Obesity has doubled since 1980. Diabetes has doubled since 1988. No one will ever be able to convince me these statistics don't mean something. I can't say for certain what foods or drinks are causing it or even if the primary cause is environmental. The fact is, that the health of our society is rapidly declining and getting worse every day. And the statistics are no different for Christians than for non-Christians. That's not how it was in the old covenant. God told the children of Israel that if they ate according to His instructions, they wouldn't get the sicknesses and diseases the pagans got. They didn't. They had amazing health.

Something is wrong. If you're counting on the world to provide you with healthy food so that, as a result, you will be healthy, you are sadly mistaken. If you think you can go on a diet of fruits and vegetables and have the divine health described in the Bible, you will be disappointed. It just doesn't work. There are too many factors working against you.

What are you to do? You must eat. And God promised you divine health under the new covenant. How can you have divine health when you eat what were once unclean foods? How can you have divine health when you eat man-made chemically processed and packaged foods that have been genetically modified from how God created them? And how can you have divine health when every time you put a bite of food in your mouth, there is the potential for deadly contamination?

Jesus told us how.

JESUS DIET PRINCIPLE #3

Always say a prayer of thanksgiving before you eat, and the food and drink will become consecrated and beneficial for your body.

Jesus was the first person to say a prayer of thanksgiving before eating. There is no instruction in Old Testament law to pray before you eat. The only thing similar is found in Deuteronomy 8:10 which says, "When you have eaten and are full, then you shall bless the Lord your God for the good land which He has given you." They were to pray and thank God after they ate. Jesus always gave thanks before He ate:

> Then He commanded the multitudes to sit down on the grass. And He took the five loaves and the two fish, and looking up to heaven, He blessed and broke and gave the loaves to the disciples; and the disciples gave to the multitudes. (Matthew 14:19)

> Then he took the seven loaves and the fish, and when he had given thanks, he broke them and gave them to the disciples, and they in turn to the people. (Matthew 15:36 NIV)

> Now it came to pass, as He sat at the table with them, that He took bread, blessed and broke it, and gave it to them. (Luke 24:30)

At the Lord's Supper, Jesus gave thanks twice, once when He took the cup and again when He broke the bread.

Read Luke 22:17–19:

> Then He took the cup, and gave thanks, and said, "Take this and divide it among yourselves; for I say to you, I will not drink of the fruit of the vine until the kingdom of God comes."

> And He took bread, gave thanks and broke it, and gave it to them, saying, "This is My body which is given for you; do this in remembrance of Me."

While He was on this earth, before He put any food or drink in His mouth, He always gave thanks first. Paul followed this same pattern in Acts 27:33–36. I'm sure he learned it from the disciples and from Jesus:

> And as day was about to dawn, Paul implored them all to take food, saying, "Today is the fourteenth day you have waited and continued without food, and eaten nothing. Therefore I urge you to take nourishment, for this is for your survival, since not a hair will fall from the head of any of you." And when he had said these things, he took bread and gave thanks to God in the presence of them all; and when he had broken it he began to eat. Then they were all encouraged, and also took food themselves.

Paul was on a ship, and they were all afraid for their lives. A violent storm had come upon them, and it didn't look good. Paul wasn't worried. His response was, "Let's eat!" Before he ate, he gave thanks to God. Paul told us in 1 Timothy 4:4–5 why we give thanks before we eat our food:

> For every creature of God is good, and nothing is to be refused if it is received with thanksgiving; for it is sanctified by the word of God and prayer.

It is sanctified by the word of God and prayer! Another word for *sanctified* is consecrated. They both mean to make holy. Food is sanctified in the new covenant if it is received with thanksgiving. Do you remember that in the old covenant, food was sanctified by the law? Reread Leviticus 11:44–47:

> For I am the Lord your God. You shall therefore consecrate yourselves, and you shall be holy; for I am holy. Neither shall you defile yourselves with any creeping thing that creeps on the earth. For I am the Lord who brings you up out of the land of Egypt, to be your God. You shall therefore be holy, for I am holy.

This is the law of the animals and the birds and every living creature that moves in the waters, and of every creature that creeps
on the earth, to distinguish between the unclean and the clean,
and between the animal that may be eaten and the animal that
may not be eaten.

How did you consecrate yourself (v.44)? By eating what was clean.
That was what made you holy, and what made food good for you to
eat. In the new covenant, what makes food clean and holy is a
prayer of thanksgiving before it's eaten.

When Jesus ate, it literally became an act of worship. He thanked
God for the provision of the food, but He blessed the food so it
would become clean and set apart for His use, namely the nourishment of His body. The food itself was not holy, but Jesus made it
holy by receiving it with thanksgiving.

When the food and drink are sanctified, something miraculous
occurs. Food that is unclean and bad for you becomes clean. Then it
becomes useful to your body even if it was unclean and not the best
choice. Food with contaminants and impurities become purified,
and you are protected from the harm the food could cause. Do you
believe that? Does that sound too far-fetched? Before Jesus ascended
into heaven, He said this to His disciples in Mark 16:16–18 (NIV):

Whoever believes and is baptized will be saved, but whoever does
not believe will be condemned. And these signs will accompany
those who believe: In my name they will drive out demons; they
will speak in new tongues; they will pick up snakes with their
hands; **and when they drink deadly poison**, it will not hurt them
at all; they will place their hands on sick people, and they will get
well. (Emphasis Added)

They will drink deadly poison, and it will not hurt them at all!
How is that possible? The only way was for God to miraculously
change the chemical properties of the poison so it would not harm
their bodies. Jesus didn't tell them to go and drink deadly poison.

He was warning them they were going to be persecuted. Someone might make them drink a deadly poison. He told them not to worry about it. If they drank deadly poison, it wouldn't hurt them because God would protect them.

I believe God will protect us when we eat foods that are unclean, or He would have never told us it was okay to eat them.

In Luke 10:8, Jesus told the disciples that when entering a city, if welcomed, they should "eat whatever is set before you." They didn't have to worry about eating foods that might have been tainted or unhealthy. Paul said the same thing in 1 Corinthians 10:25–27:

> Eat whatever is sold in the meat market, asking no questions for conscience' sake; for "the earth is the Lord's, and all its fullness."

> If any of those who do not believe invites you to dinner, and you desire to go, eat whatever is set before you, asking no question for conscience' sake.

Eat whatever is set before you. I realize Paul was talking about meat previously unclean. However, it applies to us today. If someone invites you to dinner, eat whatever they put before you. Don't worry about it. Just give thanks first.

I had stomach problems for years when I ate certain foods. If I avoided the foods, my stomach didn't bother me. If I ate the foods, it would. I know what you are thinking: just don't eat those foods! But I like them and want to eat them occasionally. When I began to understand the principles of the Jesus Diet, I became convinced that if I received those foods with thanksgiving, they would not bother my stomach anymore. That is exactly what happened! When I ate the foods that used to bother me, if I sincerely gave thanks first, they no longer bothered my stomach. If I didn't, they did bother me. The prayer of thanksgiving changed the effect the food had on my body.

Before you summarily reject that statement, think about all the times Jesus miraculously changed the physical chemistry of food. He turned water into wine. He fed five thousand men, in addition to an unknown number of women and children, with five loaves of bread and two fish. He fed four thousand men, plus women and children, with seven loaves and a few fish. Before He fed the multitudes, He looked up to heaven, gave thanks, and then broke the bread. The miracle transformation of the food happened immediately after the giving of thanks.

Jesus followed the same routine when He raised Lazarus from the dead. Read John 11: 40–44 (NIV):

Then Jesus said, "Did I not tell you that if you believe, you will see the glory of God?"

So they took away the stone. Then Jesus looked up and said, "Father, I thank you that you have heard me. I knew that you always hear me, but I said this for the benefit of the people standing here, that they may believe that you sent me."

When he had said this, Jesus called in a loud voice, "Lazarus, come out!" The dead man came out, his hands and feet wrapped with strips of linen, and a cloth around his face.

Jesus said to them, "Take off the grave clothes and let him go."

Jesus looked up to heaven and thanked God for hearing His prayer and miraculously raising Lazarus from the dead. He looked up to heaven, thanked God for the food, blessed it, and it was miraculously multiplied. When we thank God before we eat and receive our food with thanksgiving, it becomes sanctified by God, and a miracle occurs. That explains why we can eat food that is unclean. God would never tell us to eat food that is unclean and bad for us without doing something to make sure it won't harm us.

I know. That's hard to believe. You may think what I'm saying is you can eat a piece of chocolate cake and, if you give thanks beforehand, it miraculously is going to have the same effect on your body as broccoli. Sort of. But it's not as simple as that. Read 1 Corinthians 10:27–30:

> If someone who isn't a believer asks you home for dinner, accept the invitation if you want to. Eat whatever is offered to you without raising questions of conscience. (But suppose someone tells you, "This meat was offered to an idol." Don't eat it, out of consideration for the conscience of the one who told you. It might not be a matter of conscience for you, but it is for the other person). For why should my freedom be limited by what someone else thinks? If I can thank God for the food and enjoy it, why should I be condemned for eating it?

Verse thirty is an amazing statement that capsulizes everything I'm saying in this chapter: If I thank God for the food, why shouldn't I eat it and enjoy it. The disciples and Paul had a clear understanding that giving thanks before they ate food was beneficial to them. They got that teaching from Jesus. If someone invites you to their house and has cakes and donuts and all kinds of foods that would not be considered healthy, eat it anyway and enjoy it. Just give thanks first. Food is consecrated and set apart for your use when you give thanks, even if it is chocolate cake or a donut.

The Bible doesn't specifically say God changes the composition of food when we give thanks, before we eat it. However, follow the logic. God made all foods clean. Unclean foods are not healthy for us to eat, but they are consecrated when we receive them with thanksgiving, which means they are set apart as holy for us to eat by the word of God and by prayer. The word of God is Jesus declaring all foods clean, and prayer is our expression of thanksgiving. Those two things make the food consecrated.

God promises us divine health in the new covenant even though He told us to eat foods He knows are unhealthy for us. He told us to eat whatever is put before us even if it is unhealthy. God must do something to offset the damage the unhealthy foods do to our bodies. I believe it comes through the giving of thanks. That is a matter of faith. Your faith may lead you to a different conclusion. What is indisputable is that we are to give thanks for our food before we eat it, consecrating with our prayer.

Don't let anyone tell you that you can't eat something. Don't let anyone judge you or try to make you feel guilty about anything you drink. More importantly, don't judge yourself. Get rid of the conscience that monitors what you eat or drink. Eat or drink whatever you want. Just give thanks before you eat it, keeping in mind whether it is beneficial or not. More on that later.

First Corinthians 10:31 goes on to say in (NLT), Therefore, whether you eat or drink, or whatever you do, do all to the glory of God.

PART TWO

HONOR THE BODY OF CHRIST

CHAPTER 5
BLOOD IS THICKER THAN WATER BAPTISM

*That is why many of you are weak and sick and some have
even died.*
(1 Corinthians 11:30 NLT)

Numbers in the Bible have meaning. God wrote a whole book and called it Numbers. The number three represents wholeness and completion. God is three parts: Father, Son, and Holy Spirit. Man is three parts as well: body, soul, and spirit. Six represents man. Adam and Eve were created on the sixth day. Man had to work for six days and then rest. Seven, twelve, and seventeen represent completion. There are seven days of the week. There were twelve disciples. There were seventeen different ethnic groups represented at Pentecost. The Ten Commandments were given in seventeen verses. The Pentateuch contains 5852, or 17 x 7 x 7 x 7 + 7 + 7 + 7 verses. The 1533 verses of Genesis can be expressed as 17 x 70 + 7 x 7 x 7 or 17 x 7 + 707 + 707. The book of the Exodus contains (17 + 17) x (17 + 17) + 57, or 1213 verses. I don't know if any of that means anything, and I don't really understand it. Perhaps you do. But it is interesting, nonetheless.

Five is the number of grace. This chapter is number five, and it's about grace. That was not by design, or at least not by my design. I love it when God subtly reminds me that He is working in this book, guiding my steps even when I don't know it.

There has been disagreement through the centuries as to how many sacraments Christians should observe. Some churches observe seven. Some argue there should be three. Most practice two. The two that are universally practiced are baptism and the Lord's Supper. Those were two confirmed by Jesus.

A sacrament is a religious rite or ceremony. Those are religious terms that I don't necessarily like. You will see later in this chapter that I don't view the Lord's Supper as either a religious rite or ceremony. It has been relegated to that status in our churches today, and I think that contributes to our health problems, as you will soon see.

The sacraments are viewed as mostly symbolic. That is another problem. I am not sure the Lord's Supper is meant to be as symbolic as we think. Christians believe and practice that baptism is a symbolic identification with the death and resurrection of Jesus Christ, and it is. Just as Christ was buried in the grave for three days (Romans 6:3), a believer is buried with Christ in the waters of baptism and raised to walk in newness of life (Romans 6:4). As Christ died for our sins, symbolically, our sins are washed away in baptism.

In the Old Testament, water sometimes symbolized salvation, and Noah's Ark was a representation of baptism as eight people were saved from the flood. Even in the Mosaic law, the priests were commanded to do an external cleansing before they performed their priestly duties. The prophets Isaiah and Ezekiel, and even David used water as an external symbol of internal cleansing.

It was not called baptism until the New Testament. John the Baptist "baptized" his followers with a baptism of repentance. Not for the remission of sins, which can only come through Christ, but it was a foreshadowing of the baptism to come through Christ. Jesus, of course, was baptized by John the Baptist in the Jordan River. He had no need for cleansing from sins, but still modeled the importance of baptism for believers. His disciples were taught to baptize believers immediately after they were saved, and that practice continued with the early church and to this day.

I had the privilege of baptizing more than sixty-five people, including my wife, in the Jordan River near where Jesus was baptized. They were already believers who wanted to experience baptism in that unique setting. It was one of the highlights of my life, watching the elation of each person who had an obvious encounter with God in the waters. It was exciting to be baptized near the same spot as Jesus. Even though baptism is symbolic, it is highly meaningful to the believer. It's like an identification. I wear a wedding ring because I want the world to know I am married. I'm baptized as a public proclamation of my identification with Christ. I want the world to know I am a Christian.

Jesus instituted the Lord's Supper the night before His crucifixion. It's generally called communion in today's churches. Like baptism, communion is considered a largely symbolic act. That's a major error in the body of Christ today. Read what Paul said in 1 Corinthians 11:30 (NLT):

That is why many of you are weak and sick and some have even died.

Why were they weak, sick, and dying? He starts the verse by saying "That" is why many of you are weak and sick and dying. Are you curious to know what "that" is? When I started studying this verse, I was very curious. It got my attention. I want to know why people are weak, sick, and dying. Let's look at the full context of the passage and then we will break it down verse by verse. It is very enlightening:

When you meet together, you are not really interested **in the Lord's Supper**. For some of you hurry to eat your own meal without sharing with others. As a result, some go hungry while others get drunk. What? Don't you have your own homes for eating and drinking? Or do you really want to disgrace God's church and shame the poor? What am I supposed to say? Do you want me to praise you? Well, I certainly will not praise you for this!

For I pass on to you what **I received from the Lord** himself. On the night when he was betrayed, the Lord Jesus took some bread and gave thanks to God for it. Then he broke it in pieces and said, "This is my body, which is given for you. Do this in remembrance of me." In the same way, he took the cup of wine after supper, saying, "This cup is the new covenant between God and his people—an agreement confirmed with my blood. Do this in remembrance of me **as often as you drink it.**" For every time you eat this bread and drink this cup, you are announcing the Lord's death until he comes again.

So anyone who eats this bread or drinks this cup of the Lord unworthily is guilty of sinning against the body and blood of the Lord. That is why you should examine yourself before eating the bread and drinking the cup. For if you eat the bread or drink the cup without **honoring the body of Christ**, you are eating and drinking God's judgment upon yourself. **That is why many of you are weak and sick and some have even died.**

But if we would examine ourselves, we would not be judged by God in this way. Yet when we are judged by the Lord, we are being disciplined so that we will not be condemned along with the world.

So, my dear brothers and sisters, when you gather for the Lord's Supper, wait for each other. If you are really hungry, eat at home so you won't bring judgment upon yourselves when you meet together. (1 Corinthians 11:20–34 NLT) (Emphasis added)

This entire passage deals with how the church of Corinth was practicing the Lord's Supper. Paul admonished them for doing it wrong. In verse twenty, he said they weren't really interested in the Lord's Supper. They were meeting together and having a meal, but they were not focused on the Lord's Supper as much as on the eating and drinking. Because they were doing it wrong, they were weak, sick, and dying. How can something that is mostly symbolic, and nothing more than a religious rite or ceremony, cause an entire church to be weak, sick, and dying? Let's see why.

THIS REVELATION CAME DIRECTLY FROM JESUS

For I pass on to you what I received from the Lord himself. (v. 23)

First, you need to understand that this instruction came directly from Jesus. Paul said He was passing on what He received from the Lord himself. Paul made it clear that he wasn't expressing his own opinions. Everything Paul wrote in the Bible was inspired by the Holy Spirit, but he noted that this principle came from a supernatural revelation given to him through a personal encounter with Jesus.

I read these passages as words directly from Jesus. In verses twenty-four and twenty-five, Paul recounted what happened the night Jesus instituted the Lord's Supper. Jesus told Paul verbatim what He did and said the night He shared the Lord's Supper with His disciples. What's written here mirrors accounts recorded by the disciples in Matthew 26, Mark 14, and Luke 22. Perhaps Paul had already been told the account from the disciples, or maybe he was learning the specifics for the first time. Either way, the specific revelations for the church of Corinth were new. They were not celebrating the Lord's Supper with the attitude and spirit in which it was intended.

THE REASON THEY WERE WEAK, SICK, AND DYING

For if you eat the bread or drink the cup without honoring the body of Christ, you are eating and drinking God's judgment upon yourself. That is why many of you are weak and sick and some have even died. (v. 29–30)

They were eating their meal without honoring the body of Christ. That's why they were weak, sick, and dying. Here is a little background. The church of Corinth was a mess. They were fighting and into all kinds of deviant behavior. In First Corinthians chapter five, Paul said the Corinthians were into sexual immorality worse than even the pagans. That's bad when unbelievers wouldn't even do some of the things they were doing. One of them had taken his father's wife from him and, not only did the church accept it, but Paul said they were proud of him.

Sexual immorality wasn't their only problem. They would come together periodically and have a meal at least once a week but probably more often. The problem was that the rich would get there first and eat all the food and drink all the wine. When the poor arrived, there was no food or drink left. Paul even said some of them were getting drunk. Read verses 21–22:

> For some of you hurry to eat your own meal without sharing with others. As a result, some go hungry while others get drunk. What? Don't you have your own homes for eating and drinking? Or do you really want to disgrace God's church and shame the poor? What am I supposed to say? Do you want me to praise you? Well, I certainly will not praise you for this!

They were hurrying to finish their meal before the others came. There are so many different sins you could identify in their behavior. Gluttony and drunkenness were sins. A total lack of consideration for their brothers in Christ was a sin. Not sharing with others was a sin. Treating the poor as second-class Christians was a sin.

Does Paul say their sin was the reason they were weak, sick, and dying? No! He said that they were weak, sick, and dying because they were not honoring the body of Christ in the meal:

> So, anyone who eats this bread or drinks this cup of the Lord unworthily is guilty of sinning against the body and blood of the Lord. That is why you should examine yourself before eating the bread and drinking the cup. For if you eat the bread or drink the cup without honoring the body of Christ, you are eating and

drinking God's judgment upon yourself. That is why many of you are weak and sick and some have even died. (vs. 27-30)

They were guilty of sinning against the body and blood of the Lord. They were eating and drinking unworthily. While the Lord's Supper is to be a time of remembrance and reflection on the death of Jesus, they were totally disregarding its true meaning and focusing on satisfying their appetites.

Paul said they should examine themselves before eating the bread and drinking the cup. Examine themselves for what? Most have interpreted that to mean they should have examined themselves to see if there was any sin in them. That was not what Paul was saying. They should have examined themselves before eating the meal to make sure they were giving proper consideration to its meaning.

The judgment was poor health. The judgment was not for their sin. There is no more judgment for sin. Christ has already paid that judgment. However, if you dishonor the body and blood of Christ when you eat, you bring the judgment of sickness upon your body.

We partake of the Lord's Supper because we already know we sin. The Lord's Supper is not a time to reflect on our sin, but a time to remember that Christ died for our sin. In the new covenant, our sin is no longer the issue. However, our reverence for and honoring the body of Christ and the sacrifice of the broken body and shed blood is everything in the new covenant.

HOW DO YOU HONOR THE BODY OF CHRIST?

The word *honor* means to pay respect and to place value upon. Other translations use the word "discern," as in, "Discern the body of Christ." Discern means to investigate and reach a decision. It literally means to decide. To discern and honor properly the body of Christ means to investigate, judge, and decide for yourself that the body of Christ should be respected and valued.

At the Last Supper, Jesus told His disciples the meaning of the bread as the body of Christ and He told Paul its meaning again in this passage in First Corinthians. The bread represents His body, which was broken for us. The cup represents His blood. When Christ went to the cross, His body was broken for us, and His blood was shed for us. His body was broken for our physical healing, and His blood was shed for the forgiveness of our sins. If you are not honoring and discerning the body of Christ, you are not recognizing and valuing that, when Jesus's body was broken, He secured for you the healing of your body and His shed blood covered your sins. Read 1 Peter 2:24 and Matthew 8:17:

> Who Himself bore our sins in His own body on the tree, that we, having died to sins, might live for righteousness—by whose stripes you were healed.

> He Himself took our infirmities and bore our sicknesses.

REMEMBER JESUS

Jesus said to "do this in remembrance of me." What are we to remember? We are to remember that His body was broken for our physical healing and His blood was shed for the forgiveness of our sins. The Lord's Supper is to be in remembrance of what Christ did. I can see how coming together for a meal and focusing on eating and drinking with little or no regard for what Jesus did on the cross could be offensive to Christ. His sacrifice was so great. Is it really that hard for us to take a few moments before we eat and thank God for the provision of the food and then honor His sacrifice on the cross for our healing and our salvation?

If dishonoring the body of Christ resulted in them being weak, sick and dying prematurely, wouldn't the opposite also be true? Wouldn't honoring the body of Christ result in you being strong, healthy, and living a long life?

WE ARE ALSO WEAK SICK AND DYING PREMATURELY

We have the same problem today in the body of Christ. We have many among us who are weak, sick, and dying prematurely. There is no need for me to cite the statistics again. We all know what they are.

We mistakenly believe the reason we have so many health problems is because of our poor diets. That's not the reason. Jesus didn't say to the church of Corinth that they were sick because they ate too much. He didn't say that drunkenness was causing them to die young. We have focused on the wrong thing. The body of Christ is having its physical issues because of the way we have basically ignored the Lord's Supper. For us, it's a religious rite we do occasionally at church. We do it all wrong. Here is what we can learn from this passage:

A. THE LORD'S SUPPER IS A MEAL

The Lord's Supper was the final meal Jesus shared with His disciples before His death and resurrection. It was the Passover meal, which was a feast celebrated annually by the Jews to commemorate the deliverance from Egypt:

> For I pass on to you what I received from the Lord himself. On the night when he was betrayed, the Lord Jesus took some bread and **gave thanks** to God for it. Then he broke it in pieces and said, "This is my body, which is given for you. Do this in remembrance of me." In the same way, he took the cup of wine **after supper**, saying, "This cup is the new covenant between God and his people—an agreement confirmed with my blood. Do this in remembrance of me as often as you drink it." (1 Corinthians 11: 23–25 NLT)

While they were eating, Jesus took bread, and when he had **given thanks**, he broke it and gave it to his disciples, saying, "Take and eat; this is my body." (Matthew 26:26 NIV)

Likewise, He also took the cup **after supper**, saying, "This cup is the new covenant in My blood, which is shed for you. (Luke 22:20) (Emphasis Added)

The Lord's Supper was not a rite or ritual that was separate from the meal. Notice Jesus broke the bread "while they were eating" (Matthew 26:26). He didn't immediately do the cup. It says they finished eating and, "after supper," Jesus took the cup and said it was the new covenant in His blood. During the normal course of the meal, Jesus took the opportunity to explain to them the meaning of the Lord's Supper, or more specifically, to explain the meaning of His death, which was about to take place.

In Corinthians, the Lord's Supper was a part of the community meal:

When you meet together, you are not really interested in the Lord's Supper. For some of you hurry to eat your own meal without sharing with others. As a result, some go hungry while others get drunk. (1 Corinthians 11: 20–21 NLT)

The Lord's Supper was not a separate ritual. It says they "hurried their own meal." They were coming together to eat, and they considered that meal "breaking bread" and partaking of the Lord's Supper, just as Jesus and His disciples did.

Their church was not like our church today. They got together in homes and had meals together. It wasn't a building with a formal service. Almost every time they came together, a meal was involved. They didn't separate the Lord's Supper from that meal. It was all the same thing. They had the understanding that when they broke bread, they were to honor the body of Christ. When they drank wine, they were to remember the shed blood of Christ. The whole meal was a commemoration of the finished works of Christ on the cross.

B. WE SHOULD PARTAKE OF THE LORDS SUPPER OFTEN

For I pass on to you what I received from the Lord himself. On the night when he was betrayed, the Lord Jesus took some bread and gave thanks to God for it. Then he broke it in pieces and said, "This is my body, which is given for you. Do this in remembrance of me."

In the same way, he took the cup of wine after supper, saying, "This cup is the new covenant between God and his people—an agreement confirmed with my blood. Do this in remembrance of me as **often** as you drink it." For every time you eat this bread and drink this cup, you are announcing the Lord's death until he comes again. (1 Corinthians 11:23–26 NLT) (Emphasis Added)

> Jesus said, "Do this in remembrance of me as **often** as you drink it." He went on to say, "For **every** time you eat this bread and drink this cup, you are announcing the Lord's death until He comes again." I take this to mean that every time you eat a meal, and as often as you eat and drink anything, you should do it in remembrance of Christ.

"As often as you drink it" could be interpreted one of two ways. It could mean as often as you come together as a church, you should take the Lord's Supper as a meal, or it could mean that every time you eat or drink anything, corporate or otherwise, you should do it in remembrance of Christ. Most churches today are not doing either.

JESUS DIET PRINCIPLE #4
Honor the body of Christ often.

The Bible does not give clear instructions on how often we are to take the Lord's Supper other than "as often as," which could be interpreted differently. The term "breaking bread" is used five times in the book of Acts. Breaking bread was a Jewish term that meant the eating of a meal. It did not necessarily mean the Lord's Supper to the Jews, but it seems to mean that to the disciples. Breaking bread was clearly associated with Jesus. When Jesus fed the multitudes, He broke the bread. When He instituted the Lord's Supper, He broke the bread and said that it was His body broken for us. The disciples recognized Jesus in Luke 24:35, from the way in which He "broke bread."

There was no clear pattern as to when and how often the early church broke bread. In Acts 2:42–46, Scripture says they broke bread daily in their homes. In the early church, they were together sharing a meal every day, sometimes several times a day. They may very well have observed the Lord's Supper every time they shared a meal. They may not have. We just don't know. There were some early theologians who concluded, based on Acts 2:42–46, the observance of the Lord's Supper was once a day at the main meal.

Some Scriptures in Acts say that they broke bread together on the first day of the week. This signifies a corporate meal. On the first day of the week, they came together for worship, prayer, and the partaking of the Lord's Supper. It was still observed during the course of a meal; it was just done once a week as a part of their worship experience. Acts 27:35, describes Paul eating a meal and "breaking bread." This was among unbelievers. There was no corporate worship involved. Paul was sharing a meal with the sailors on the ship who were tasked with taking him to trial. He gave thanks and then broke bread.

It's not clear that the breaking of the bread in these passages was the observance of the Lord's Supper. What is clear is that every time they ate a meal, corporate or otherwise, they gave thanks beforehand, just as Jesus modeled for them, and they had an awareness of Christ in the meal. For the disciples, the breaking of bread reminded them of the times they broke bread with Christ. For Paul, it was a remembrance of the body and blood of Christ as Jesus had taught the disciples. I believe that every time they sat down to eat bread, they must have remembered Jesus teaching that it was His broken body. Every time they took a drink from the cup, there must have been a sense of Jesus's teaching that it was representative of His blood shed for them. That's the essence of the Lord's Supper. It is the honoring of Christ's body and blood and the remembrance of His finished works on our behalf.

I take the Lord's Supper with every meal. I take time with each meal to remember Jesus. I don't think I must wait until we do it together as a church. My church does it four or five times a year. That's not often enough for me. And what is the church? After all, isn't my body the Temple of the Holy Spirit? Doesn't the Bible teach we are all the "church," members of one body? Doesn't Scripture say when two or more are gathered together, He is in their midst? When my wife and I eat a meal together, aren't we both members of the body of Christ, with the Holy Spirit present in our midst? What could possibly be wrong with our taking time to thank God for the food, and pausing a moment to remember the finished works of Christ on the cross?

I have no problem with you interpreting this in your own way since Scripture is not fully clear. It might not be clear because God, in this new covenant of grace, is not going to establish a law we must follow. It's a matter of your heart. What is clear is that it is to be often and meaningful.

If you only took communion when your church did, it probably wouldn't be very often. I know that's not right. Most churches rarely have a meal together, and when they do, they almost never incorporate communion into it. If you want to make the argument that the Lord's Supper was meant only for when you get together as the church, then do that. I implore churches: start doing communion often. You aren't doing communion regularly when you meet corporately. You aren't eating meals together as a church very often, and when you do, the Lord's Supper is rarely observed. And you aren't doing the Lord's Supper every time you are together, at meals or otherwise. If you were, your congregations wouldn't be so weak, sick, and dying.

I read some arguments that if you do the Lord's Supper too often, it loses its meaning. I think the opposite is true. It has lost its meaning because we do it so irregularly. I love that I am doing it every day. Several times a day, I'm remembering that Christ died on the cross for my sicknesses and my sins. I think God, in His brilliance, tied our divine health to giving thanks at each meal and honoring the body of Christ so that we would be remembering Him often. I eat two or three times a day. By the giving of thanks and the Lord's Supper at each meal, God ensures that I am taking time each day to remember Him.

You discern for yourself what you should do. You can investigate and read the Scriptures and judge for yourself. Just start regularly partaking of the Lord's Supper. Keep in mind that the principles of the Jesus Diet are not laws. We are not creating an old covenant law that you must follow religiously, or God won't bless you. However, if you aren't honoring the Lord's body, you are opening yourself up to the potential judgment of sickness and disease.

I hope you are convinced that every time you eat, you honor the body of Christ. I don't see how that could ever hurt you. It might make the difference in your health. It has in mine.

CHAPTER 6
DO YOU SEE YOUR SHADOW?

Let no man therefore judge you in meat, or in drink, or in respect of
an holy day, or of the new moon, or of the sabbath days: Which are
a shadow of things to come; but the body is of Christ.
(Colossians 2:16–17 KJV)

Punxsutawney Phil is a famous groundhog that lives in Punxsutawney, Pennsylvania. Once a year, on February 2, Phil emerges
from hibernation, with much fanfare, from his temporary home
known as Gobblers Knob. If Phil sees his shadow, it means six more
weeks of winter. If Phil doesn't see his shadow, there will be an early
spring. The entire day is known as Groundhog Day.

Have you ever wondered how they know Phil saw his shadow?
After Phil is awakened from his deep sleep, he tells the president of
the Groundhog Club (known as the Inner Circle) the results. I
didn't know groundhogs could speak. Apparently, they can. They
speak what is known as Groundhogese. The president is the only
person who speaks Groundhogese and can understand what Phil is
saying. I think the whole thing is a sham. The results are actually determined by the Inner Circle before Phil emerges from his home.

It's a nationally televised event. Millions of people tune in to see
the results. Years ago, farmers planted their crops based on what the
groundhog said was going to happen. If I was a farmer, I don't think

I would want my livelihood based on a silly superstition. They don't anymore. Turns out, Phil does not have a very good track record. It is estimated he has been right about thirty-five to forty percent of the time. Since it is only a guess, they should be right at least fifty percent of the time! They must not be very good guessers.

The tradition dates to 1887 and originates from a pagan superstition. In the old days, it was a bear, not a groundhog. Ancient Europeans believed bears were to be worshiped and that weather was controlled by bears. Bears were prophets, and when they came out of hibernation in the spring, they predicted the future weather. I think the president of the Inner Circle just prefers to hold up a groundhog rather than a bear. Seems safer.

We are very superstitious people. Walking under a ladder is said to be bad luck. So is breaking a mirror and seeing a black cat. In Egypt, seeing a black cat is considered good luck. I'm not sure which is correct. I'm guessing neither. I don't like cats, so I prefer not to see a cat of any color. You shouldn't step on a crack in the sidewalk, because you will break your mother's back. I have stepped on many cracks in the sidewalk, even on purpose, and my mom was just fine.

It's amazing how many of our traditions come from pagan superstitions. If you spill salt, you're supposed to throw more salt over your shoulder. The idea is that the devil is always behind you. When you throw salt over your shoulder, it gets in his eyes and temporarily blinds him so he can't distract you. A rabbit's foot comes from an ancient belief that a rabbit is a god of fertility. I guess it's because rabbits procreate so vigorously. Carrying around the rabbit's foot is supposed to bring good luck. It wasn't very good luck for the rabbit who is missing a foot! If rabbits were gods, shouldn't they be able to keep us from cutting off their feet? I'm just saying.

We say, "God bless you," when someone sneezes. That would seem like a nice, Christian, and polite thing to say. The ancient pagan belief is when you sneeze, your soul escapes from your body. "God bless you" is a pagan prayer asking your soul to come back.

Knocking on wood, crossing your fingers, and picking up a penny are all supposed to bring you good luck. Our two poodles are named Lucky and Penny. The saying goes, "See a penny, pick it up, and all day long, you'll have good luck." They weren't named for that saying. My wife's grandparents had a dog named Lucky and another named Penny. I don't know if the saying applies to Penny the poodle or if it is just coins, but I pick Penny up all the time and I have never noticed any better luck. I've always believed my luck comes from God.

Another superstition says bird droppings falling on your head is good luck. It's supposed to be a sign wealth is coming your way. I think anytime a bird drops poop on my head, it is not a good day! I think I prefer to make money the old-fashioned way and just earn it. Putting your purse on the ground is supposed to be bad luck. The saying goes, "A purse on the floor is money out the door." My wife needs to be aware of that one. She is always putting her purse on the floor.

Thirteen is considered an unlucky number in the United States. This belief has been classified a phobia, called Triskaidekaphobia. Say that word three times in a row. I was in an office building the other day that didn't have a thirteenth floor. Many hotels don't either because people don't want to stay on that floor. Isn't the fourteenth floor really the thirteenth? Are we just fooling ourselves about something so stupid?

Friday the thirteenth is considered a day to be careful in America. In China, four is the unlucky number. Many Chinese hotels and office buildings don't have a fourth floor. They really have a fourth floor; they just call it the fifth floor. In Italy, Friday the seventeenth is considered unlucky. In Russia, an even number is unlucky. If you give roses to your significant other, she will be offended if they are an even number of roses. No dozen roses in Russia! And don't make them yellow. Yellow signifies infidelity. You will be in a lot of trouble if you send her a dozen yellow roses. It signifies to her you were unfaithful and are apologizing. I have sent my wife a dozen yellow roses many times—and not for that reason. She always seems to love them.

A superstition in China is you shouldn't sleep with your head facing north. It's bad luck. In Africa, it's bad luck to sleep facing west. We're running out of options! I hope no cultures think sleeping facing south or east is bad luck, or we are in trouble. In one culture, it's bad luck to get your haircut on Tuesday. In Thailand, haircuts on Wednesdays are bad luck. In some places, it's considered bad luck to go to bed with wet hair. One superstition says it will make you go blind.

Don't wash your hair the day before a test. Superstition says it will wash out the learning you got from studying. I wish I had known that when I showed my parents my report cards. I could have blamed it on them. "It's not my fault! You made me take a shower the day before my test!"

In France, if you step in dog poop with your left foot, it's good luck. If you step in it with your right foot, It's bad luck. I wonder if some people step on poop on purpose with their left foot just to change their luck. I think anytime I step in dog poop, it's bad luck. It's considered bad luck to enter a room leading with your left foot. What if you have just stepped in dog poop with your left foot? That is good luck. If you walk in the room leading with your left foot, did you cancel out the good luck you got from the dog poop? You will have a mess on the floor either way. It is definitely bad luck for the person who has to clean it off the floor and off your shoe.

In Korea, it's bad luck for a pregnant woman to eat asymmetrical food. It is said that if she eats unshapely food, she will have an ugly baby. In Japan, it's bad luck to trim your nails at night. It's more than bad luck. It can cause premature death! Have you heard this one? Don't kiss a baby on the lips. You will condemn him or her to a lifetime of drooling. I drool sometimes at night on my pillow. I wonder who kissed me on the lips when I was a kid! It must have been my aunt Gertrude. Come to think of it, she was not very pretty. Her mother must have eaten asymmetrical food when she was pregnant! She didn't live very long either. I wonder if she trimmed her nails at night!

There are many superstitions related to shadows. I already mentioned the groundhog. Many cultures believe your shadow is a representation of your soul. The ancient Greeks believed if you lost your shadow, you would die. Others believe shadows are evil spirits. Have you ever heard the phrase, "He is afraid of his own shadow"? That's where the saying came from. I wonder if the writer of Peter Pan was thinking about that superstition when Peter lost his shadow and Wendy had to sew it back on.

I don't believe in superstitions. To me, every superstition sounds too foolish to believe. I don't believe a groundhog can predict the weather. I don't think anything can bring me bad luck other than my own stupid behavior. Then it's not bad luck. I do believe in shadows, but I'm not afraid of them. At least, I believe in the shadows in the Bible. Those are good things. Colossians 2 and Hebrews 10 say the law is a shadow of Christ.

The word "shadow" means a sketch of or an outline of. It's a resemblance, but not the real thing. You could look at it this way. It is an imperfect representation of the real thing. That's not unlike our own shadows. They are reflections of the real thing, not unlike a mirror, but they are not real in and of themselves. In the Bible, shadows are real; they are just imperfect.

There are many shadows of Christ in the Old Testament: Isaac was to be sacrificed on the altar by his father, Abraham; Christ was sacrificed on the cross by His Father. Jonah was in the belly of a whale for three days; Jesus was in the grave for three days. Noah's ark is a shadow of Christ in that Noah and his family were safe and protected from the flood while inside the ark. Christ is like the ark. We are in Christ and are protected from destruction. In the old covenant, a lamb without blemish was sacrificed for the sins of the people; Christ was without sin and is called the Lamb of God. He was sacrificed for our sins.

The Passover is a shadow of the Lord's Supper. The Passover was instituted the night before the children of Israel were led out of Egypt. They had been slaves for more than four hundred years. God called Moses to deliver them from Egypt, but Pharaoh refused to let them go. Several horrible plagues came upon the Egyptians, and yet Pharaoh refused to listen to God and let His people go. God said the last plague would be that the first born of every family would die.

However, God made a provision for the children of Israel. He told them to sacrifice a lamb and put its blood above the door of their house. The angel of death would pass them by, and they would be saved (Exodus 12:22–23). He also gave them instructions to eat a meal:

> Then they shall eat the flesh on that night; roasted in fire, with unleavened bread and with bitter herbs they shall eat it. Do not eat it raw, nor boiled at all with water, but roasted in fire—its head with its legs and its entrails. You shall let none of it remain until morning, and what remains of it until morning you shall burn with fire. And thus you shall eat it: with a belt on your waist, your sandals on your feet, and your staff in your hand. So, you shall eat it in haste. It is the **Lord's Passover**. (Exodus 12:8–11) (Emphasis Added)

It was called "the Lord's Passover." Two things happened the night of the Lord's Passover. First, they were completely protected from death. There was not a single Egyptian household where there was not one dead, including Pharaoh's firstborn son. Not one of the first born of the children of Israel died:

> And it came to pass at midnight that the Lord struck all the first-born in the land of Egypt, from the firstborn of Pharaoh who sat on his throne to the firstborn of the captive who was in the dun-

geon, and all the firstborn of livestock. So Pharaoh rose in the night, he, all his servants, and all the Egyptians; and there was a great cry in Egypt, for there was not a house where there was not one dead. (Exodus 12:29–30)

A second miraculous thing happened that night to the children of Israel. Every single person was healed of their physical infirmities and diseases:

He also brought them out with silver and gold, and there was none feeble among His tribes. (Psalm 105:37)

There were more than 600,000 men, not including women and children, who came out of Egypt. Not one of them was feeble! How was that possible? There were young people, old people, disabled people, sick people, and weak people, with every imaginable sickness in their midst. Remember, they had been slaves for many years under the worst and most unimaginable conditions. God healed them all the night of the Passover! Those who were blind were healed. Those who couldn't walk could suddenly walk. Broken bones were healed. People who were bedridden could get up and walk out of Egypt. It didn't matter how old or how young you were; you were not feeble anymore. Suddenly, you were renewed. You had all the strength you needed to walk out of Egypt and into the desert. The route of the Exodus was 520 miles long counting the years wandering in the wilderness. That journey would have been impossible with sick and disabled people. Yet none were feeble, and all were up for the journey.

The Lord's Passover doesn't sound symbolic to me. There were real manifestations of miracles in their lives. They were protected from death by the blood and healed from every sickness and disease by the breaking of the bread.

God commanded the children of Israel to observe the Passover once a year:

> And you shall observe this thing as an ordinance for you and your sons forever. It will come to pass when you come to the land which the Lord will give you, just as He promised, that you shall keep this service. And it shall be, when your children say to you, 'What do you mean by this service?' that you shall say, 'It is the Passover sacrifice of the Lord, who passed over the houses of the children of Israel in Egypt when He struck the Egyptians and delivered our households.'" So, the people bowed their heads and worshiped. Then the children of Israel went away and did so; just as the Lord had commanded Moses and Aaron, so they did. (Exodus 12: 24-28)

Jesus and His disciples were having their Passover meal when Jesus instituted the Lord's Supper. Notice the similarities in the Lord's Passover and the Lord's Supper. The Lord's Passover consisted of eating unleavened bread and the flesh of the lamb slain for their salvation. The Lord's Supper consisted of breaking the bread that represented the body of Christ and drinking from the cup that represented the blood of Christ. Both brought physical healing and salvation to God's people.

That was by design. Jesus is the fulfillment of the Lord's Passover. Notice that the Lord's Passover was called "the Passover sacrifice of the Lord" in verse 27. It was speaking directly of our Lord Jesus Christ. He was directly involved in the salvation and the physical healing of the children of Israel the night they were delivered out of Egypt. The Lord's Passover was the night before they were saved by the blood and healed of their sicknesses. It was no coincidence the Lord's Supper was the night before Jesus was sacrificed for our sins and physical healing. During the Passover meal, Jesus said the bread was His body and the cup held the blood of the new covenant that was shed for the remission of sins. 1 Peter 2:24 tells us Christ Himself bore on the cross our sins and our sicknesses so that we might be healed:

> "He himself bore our sins" in his body on the cross, so that we might die to sins and live for righteousness; "by his wounds you have been healed." (1 Peter 2:24 NIV)

The Passover is an imperfect representation of the real thing. The real thing is Jesus. The real thing is better than the shadow because it's perfect. Remember, the new covenant is based on better promises. The Passover was wonderful for the children of Israel, so much so that they celebrated it for 1500 years. When Jesus introduced the Lord's Supper, He was providing us with something better than the Passover.

What could be better than the Passover? In the Passover, they were all saved by the blood and completely healed by the bread. The new covenant of grace by faith is way better. Like the Passover, we are saved by the blood of Jesus, and our bodies are healed by the "Bread of Life," who is Jesus. However, in the Passover, the lamb was imperfect. The animal's blood could not save them for an eternity. Christ's blood saves us forever. The bread could bring them healing once, but they needed the Bread of Life to sustain their lives and maintain their healing. Christ's broken body provided our physical healing. All we must do is believe and remember Christ's broken body and blood when we eat our food. Then we receive the blessings of the old covenant along with the better promises of the new covenant.

THE LORD'S SUPPER IS TO BE OBSERVED FOREVER

Reread Exodus 12:24:

> And you shall observe this thing as an ordinance for you and your sons forever.

God said that the Lord's Passover was an ordinance that was to be observed forever. How is the Lord's Passover to be observed forever? We don't observe the Passover today. Or do we? We need to understand that the Lord's Supper is a continuation of the Lord's Passover just with new meaning. That's why it's so important for it to become an integral part of our lives. Jesus said we will observe the Lord's Supper with Him in the life to come:

> But I say to you, "I will not drink of this fruit of the vine from now on until that day when I drink it new with you in My Father's kingdom." (Matthew 26:29)

Jesus will eat and drink with us in the new kingdom to come. The Lord's Supper began at Passover and will continue for an eternity:

> I say to you that many will come from the east and the west and will take their places at the feast with Abraham, Isaac, and Jacob in the kingdom of heaven. (Matthew 8:11 NIV)

> Now when one of those who sat at the table with Him heard these things, he said to Him, "Blessed is he who shall eat bread in the kingdom of God!" (Luke 14:15)

We will eat bread with Jesus in the kingdom of God. We will feast with Abraham, Isaac, and Jacob. The Bible calls the Lord's Supper in the life to come "The Marriage Supper of the Lamb:"

> "Let us be glad and rejoice and give Him glory, for the marriage of the Lamb has come, and His wife has made herself ready." And to her it was granted to be arrayed in fine linen, clean and bright, for the fine linen is the righteous acts of the saints.

> Then he said to me, "Write: 'Blessed are those who are called to the marriage supper of the Lamb!'" (Revelation 19:7–9)

The Lord's Passover was observed for 1500 years. The Lord's Supper is to be observed until Jesus comes back, and then the Marriage Supper will be observed for an eternity in Heaven. We need to get back to doing our part and observing the Lord's Supper properly until Jesus comes again. The enemy would like nothing more than for us to think the Lord's Supper is symbolic. That will take away its power from manifesting in our lives. He would rather have us believe in silly superstitions. He wants us to believe things that are not true are true, and things that are true are not true. Superstitions are not true. The Lord's Supper is not just symbolism. If he can get the church to see the Lord's Supper as nothing more than a ritual or, for some, even a superstition, then it won't have any power in your life.

If you understood the power in the bread, you would do the Lord's Supper as often as you could. In the next chapter, you are going to learn the power in the bread and how it can change your life.

CHAPTER 7
WONDER BREAD

I am the bread of life. (John 6:35)

After the Lord's Passover and the salvation from the Angel of Death, the children of Israel escaped from Egypt, and God miraculously parted the waters of the Red Sea and delivered them, killing Pharaoh and all his armies. It is estimated that more than two million people came out of Egypt.

Imagine the challenge of moving that many people through the desert. It was no problem because God took full responsibility for their well-being. He not only delivered them; He sustained them:

> Now the children of Israel had done according to the word of Moses, and they had asked from the Egyptians articles of silver, articles of gold, and clothing. And the Lord had given the people favor in the sight of the Egyptians, so that they granted them what they requested. Thus, they plundered the Egyptians.

> Then the children of Israel journeyed from Rameses to Succoth, about six hundred thousand men on foot, besides children. A mixed multitude went up with them also, and flocks and herds— a great deal of livestock. (Exodus 12:35–38)

They left Egypt with an abundance of resources. The Egyptians were so afraid of the children of Israel they gave them everything. It says that they "plundered" the Egyptians. They also came out of Egypt with an ample supply of food. It says they had a great deal of livestock. This was all at God's direction through Moses.

Over time, the food began to run out. The people complained, and some even wanted to go back to Egypt. They thought slavery was better than their current state. God said He would provide them with food:

> Now it came to pass, as Aaron spoke to the whole congregation of the children of Israel, that they looked toward the wilderness, and behold, the glory of the Lord appeared in the cloud.
>
> And the Lord spoke to Moses, saying, "I have heard the complaints of the children of Israel. Speak to them, saying, 'At twilight you shall eat meat, and in the morning, you shall be filled with bread. And you shall know that I am the Lord your God.'"
>
> So it was that quail came up at evening and covered the camp, and in the morning the dew lay all around the camp. And when the layer of dew lifted, there, on the surface of the wilderness, was a small round substance, as fine as frost on the ground. So when the children of Israel saw it, they said to one another, "What is it?" For they did not know what it was.
>
> And Moses said to them, "This is the bread which the Lord has given you to eat. This is the thing which the Lord has commanded: 'Let every man gather it according to each one's need, one omer for each person, according to the number of persons; let every man take for those who are in his tent.'"
> (Exodus 16:10–16)

God gave them quail to eat at night and manna to eat in the morning. Manna was a supernatural food. The word "manna" literally means "What is it?" They didn't know what it was because they had never seen anything like it. The manna came from heaven and had supernatural properties. It sustained them for forty years:

> And the children of Israel ate manna forty years, until they came
> to an inhabited land; they ate manna until they came to the bor-
> der of the land of Canaan. (Exodus 16:35)

The result was perfect health. Look at what the Bible said about
Moses:

> Moses was one hundred and twenty years old when he died. His
> eyes were not dim, nor his natural vigor diminished.
> (Deuteronomy 34:7)

Moses lived to be 120 years old and was in perfect health. God deserves the credit. Every morsel of food he put in his mouth for forty
years came from God. How would you like to live to be 120 years old
with perfect eyesight and still as strong and vibrant as you ever
were?

It wasn't just Moses who was healthy; they all were. Caleb was
sent by Moses to spy out the promised land. The spies discovered giants in the land that would have to be defeated. Here is what Caleb
said about himself in Joshua 14:11:

> I am as strong this day as on the day that Moses sent me; just as
> my strength was then, so now is my strength for war, both for go-
> ing out and for coming in.

Some of the spies were afraid to fight the giants. Not Caleb. He
said he was as strong as he had ever been. Caleb was eighty years
old. He had eaten manna from heaven for forty years and was in
perfect health.

Notice there was nothing symbolic about the bread in the Old
Testament. Manna was real food with real life-changing properties.
Manna was the element God used to bring about divine health. God
promised them perfect health and used the Lord's Passover to heal
them initially and the manna from Heaven to maintain the healing
for forty years. It was a blessing from God:

Worship the LORD your God, and his blessing will be on your food and water. I will take away sickness from among you. (Exodus 23:25 NIV)

Where was the blessing of divine health? It was on their food and water. What does that tell us? It tells us that food and water can be changed by a blessing. Blessed food took sickness away from them. If the chemical properties of the foods were not changed when they were blessed to make it healthier, then what was the point of the blessing? If the blessing was strictly symbolic, then it had no real meaning.

It had tremendous meaning. The food and water maintained their health. It wasn't really the food and water that made them healthy; it was the blessing on the food and water that produced sickness-free living. Their part was to worship the Lord their God. In turn, God changed the physical properties of the food to give it the power to affect their health. How could it mean anything other than that God supernaturally touched the food so that it would produce divine health in them?

If you don't think that God supernaturally changes the physical composition of food, consider this point. They were told to only take one day's worth of manna and to eat all they gathered. That is because God wanted them to trust Him for their daily supply. He didn't want them saving some for the next day because it was a sign of unbelief. Look at what happened when they didn't follow God's instructions:

Notwithstanding they did not heed Moses. But some of them left part of it until morning, and it bred worms and stank. (Exodus 16:20)

The food was rotten and not edible. That manna only lasted one day. However, some manna would last for two days and not go bad:

> And so, it was, on the sixth day, that they gathered twice as much bread, two omers for each one. And all the rulers of the congregation came and told Moses. [23] Then he said to them, "This is what the Lord has said: 'Tomorrow is a Sabbath rest, a holy Sabbath to the Lord. Bake what you will bake today, and boil what you will boil; and lay up for yourselves all that remains, to be kept until morning.'" [24] So they laid it up till morning, as Moses commanded; and it did not stink, nor were there any worms in it. (Exodus 16:22–24)

That was a different instruction and the food didn't go bad. What was the difference? God changed the physical composition of the food on the sixth day so they would have provisions on the Sabbath. That was God blessing the food and supernaturally changing it based on their need.

The Bible says in Genesis 24:1 that God blessed Abraham in "all things" and Abraham became the richest man in the entire world. There was nothing symbolic in the blessing. "All things" meant things that were tangible. The Bible says God "gives the power to get wealth" (Deuteronomy 8:18). The power to get wealth is in the blessing. God supernaturally intervenes in a person's life with a blessing to give them a unique ability to get wealth. That is a power that someone without the blessing does not have.

Food that is blessed has power unblessed food does not have. That's why Jesus blessed the food before He ate it. It was not symbolic. He was literally praying for God's power to enter the food and bring life-giving properties to the food. In the feeding of the multitudes, the power was manifested in the multiplication of the food. It also strengthened them from days of not eating.

In the Lord's Supper, the power is in the transformation of the food into the body and blood of Jesus. Not that it becomes the literal body and blood of Jesus any more than the manna from heaven contained the literal physical attributes of God. But manna did contain something from heaven that made it more powerful than anything on earth. Food blessed by a prayer of thanksgiving, and food and wine that are the body and blood of Jesus, have a supernatural power that unblessed foods do not have.

Manna was a shadow of Jesus. In John 6: 30-35 (NIV), Jesus said that He was the manna from heaven that brings eternal life:

> So they asked him, "What sign then will you give that we may see it and believe you? What will you do? Our ancestors ate the manna in the wilderness; as it is written: 'He gave them bread from heaven to eat.'"

> Jesus said to them, "Very truly I tell you, it is not Moses who has given you the bread from heaven, but it is my Father who gives you the true bread from heaven. [33] For the bread of God is the bread that comes down from heaven and gives life to the world."

> "Sir," they said, "always give us this bread."

> Then Jesus declared, "I am the bread of life. Whoever comes to me will never go hungry, and whoever believes in me will never be thirsty.

Here are ways in which manna was a shadow of Jesus:

1. Both came from Heaven. The manna in the old testament was called manna from heaven. Jesus said He is the true bread from heaven.

2. Both are called bread. Manna was bread, and Jesus is called the Bread of Life.

3. Both have life-giving properties.

4. Both are free gifts from God (vs. 32 and 33).

5. Both were a sign of God's seal of approval.

Today, you can't buy manna at the grocery store. What you can buy would not be nearly as healthy for you as manna. Fortunately, you have something better. You have your own manna from heaven. It is Jesus, given to you by God as part of the new covenant. As great as manna was, it was still imperfect. They still eventually died. Jesus is the perfect manifestation of the bread. He said if you eat of the living bread, you will never die:

> I am the bread of life. Your ancestors ate the manna in the wilderness, yet they died. But here is the bread that comes down from heaven, which anyone may eat and not die. I am the living bread that came down from heaven. Whoever eats this bread will live forever. This bread is my flesh, which I will give for the life of the world. (John 6:48–51 NIV)

How do we eat the bread? By believing in Jesus. We know from John 3:16 that believing is the way we receive eternal life and live forever. Eternal life from the living bread is figurative language to draw a real comparison between the life-giving properties of manna and the eternal life provided by the Bread of Life, who is Jesus.

However, changing the physical properties of food by blessing the food is not figurative or symbolic. It is a literal manifestation of the power of God. If you worship the Lord your God by giving thanks before you eat your food, it is blessed, and the blessing changes the physical property of the food to produce divine health in you. If not, then what is the point of asking God to bless the food? It would be a waste of time. It's not a waste of time because your blessed food produces divine health in you, just like it did the children of Israel and just like it did for those who ate food blessed by Jesus. Your prayer before eating is your worship of God, and God, in turn, blesses your food for the nourishment of your body, giving the food supernatural properties.

Don't ask me to explain how food is transformed, because it is a mystery. Many things in the Bible are mysteries we will not fully understand until we get to heaven. However, the words of Jesus mean something more than symbolism:

> Jesus said to them, "Very truly I tell you, unless you eat the flesh of the Son of Man and drink his blood, you have no life in you. Whoever eats my flesh and drinks my blood has eternal life, and I will raise them up at the last day. For my flesh is real food and my blood is real drink. (John 6:53-55 NIV)

Jesus said that His flesh is "real food" and His blood is "real drink." He's talking about real food we eat and real drinks we drink. That is more than symbolic. He's trying to get us to understand that real food and real drink contains the power of His flesh and blood. When we eat food and drink the cup that is blessed by God and contains the power and life of the body and blood of Christ, we are physically healed and spiritually saved for an eternity. We are not saved by the food and drink; we are saved by the power of God. Paul said in Romans 1:16 that it is the power of God that brings salvation to everyone who believes.

The Bible almost always treats physical healing and spiritual healing as one and the same. Did you know that physical healing generally preceded salvation in the Bible? At the Lord's Passover, the children of Israel were physically healed during the meal, but they were saved from death later by the blood above the doorstep, hours after the meal was over. The same thing was true in the New Testament:

> And Ananias went his way and entered the house; and laying his hands on him he said, "Brother Saul, the Lord Jesus, who appeared to you on the road as you came, has sent me that you may receive your sight and be filled with the Holy Spirit." Immediately there fell from his eyes something like scales, and he received his sight at once; and he arose and was baptized. (Acts 9:17–18)

Ananias laid hands on Saul, and immediately, he received his sight, was saved and filled with the Holy Spirit, and then was baptized. Physical healing came before, or at least simultaneous with, spiritual healing. This same pattern was carried out by Jesus in His ministry:

> But when Jesus knew it, He withdrew from there. And great multitudes followed Him, and He healed them all. (Matthew 12:15)

> Jesus went through all the towns and villages, teaching in their synagogues, proclaiming the good news of the kingdom and healing every disease and sickness. (Matthew 9:35 NIV)

> How God anointed Jesus of Nazareth with the Holy Spirit and with power, who went about doing good and healing all who were oppressed by the devil, for God was with Him. (Acts 10:38)

> Then His fame went throughout all Syria; and they brought to Him all sick people who were afflicted with various diseases and torments, and those who were demon-possessed, epileptics, and paralytics; and He healed them. (Matthew 4:24)

> And begged Him that they might only touch the hem of His garment. And as many as touched it were made perfectly well. (Matthew: 14:36)

Jesus physically healed the sick before they were spiritually healed. There was never an instance in which someone came to Jesus wanting to be healed and He did not heal them. The only instance when it came close to happening was in Matthew 15:21–28:

> Then Jesus went out from there and departed to the region of Tyre and Sidon. And behold, a woman of Canaan came from that region and cried out to Him, saying, "Have mercy on me, O Lord, Son of David! My daughter is severely demon-possessed."

> But He answered her not a word.

> And His disciples came and urged Him, saying, "Send her away, for she cries out after us."

But He answered and said, "I was not sent except to the lost sheep of the house of Israel."

Then she came and worshiped Him, saying, "Lord, help me!"

But He answered and said, "It is not good to take the children's bread and throw it to the little dogs."

And she said, "Yes, Lord, yet even the little dogs eat the crumbs which fall from their masters' table."

Then Jesus answered and said to her, "O woman, great is your faith! Let it be to you as you desire." And her daughter was healed from that very hour.

A Gentile woman came to Jesus begging Him to heal her daughter. Jesus said that the provision was not yet available to Gentiles and He had been sent only to the lost sheep of Israel. Salvation and healing were made available to the Gentiles after Jesus's death and resurrection, but not at that time unless Jesus deviated from the plan. Jesus made a remarkable statement in verse twenty-six: Healing is the "children's bread." Here was another reference to bread, food, and physical healing. Jesus was literally saying that physical healing and salvation were like food for His children. Just as bread is food for life, salvation and physical healing are food meant for God's children.

This woman was healed because she believed in Jesus's healing power. Jesus tested her faith and said it was not good to give the children's bread to dogs. She believed even a crumb would heal her daughter. If you don't believe there is healing power in the food you eat, then it won't have any healing powers in it. If you believe blessed bread can restore your health, it will happen. Can you believe that even a crumb from bread that is blessed can restore your health? Jesus said the woman had great faith, and her daughter was healed that very hour.

You cannot separate God's provision for eternal life from His provision for abundant life on earth. You cannot separate physical healing from spiritual healing. They are meant to be one and the same. God doesn't want to spiritually heal you for an eternity but leave you physically sick for the rest of your life. For years, preachers, teachers, and writers have made the mistake of taking these passages and applying them figuratively and relating them only to eternal life. Why have we taken physical healing out of the salvation process? Why do we only preach a salvation of forgiveness of sins when God provided physical along with spiritual healing in the old covenant, and Jesus preached a salvation of physical and spiritual healing in the new covenant? The same process continued after Jesus's death:

> Also, a multitude gathered from the surrounding cities to Jerusalem, bringing sick people and those who were tormented by unclean spirits, and they were all healed. (Acts 5:16)

Once again, they were all healed. The Scriptures say again and again that everyone who was sick was healed and then they believed and began serving the Lord. Why have we gotten away from this model in our churches today?

> And believers were increasingly added to the Lord, multitudes of both men and women, so that they brought the sick out into the streets and laid them on beds and couches, that at least the shadow of Peter passing by might fall on some of them. (Acts 5:14–15)

Believers were added daily to the Lord. How were they added daily? They were being physically healed. So, the multitudes kept bringing the sick to the Apostles. They were healed, and then they became disciples of the Lord and were baptized. That wasn't the end of Jesus's provision. That was just the first step to abundant life. Just as God brought physical healing and salvation to the children of Israel, He then sustained them in the wilderness with manna from heaven. Jesus has brought physical healing and salvation to us, and He then sustains us through our entire life through His body and blood, which is the true manna from heaven that brings eternal life. Jesus has taken responsibility for our well-being from the time we are saved until the last days:

> For I have come down from heaven not to do my will but to do the will of him who sent me. And this is the will of him who sent me, that I shall lose none of all those he has given me but raise them up at the last day. (John 6: 38–39 NIV)

In the above passage, Jesus said that the Father has given Him the responsibility of gathering those who would be saved and keeping them until the last day. Just as God took responsibility for the children of Israel, Jesus has taken responsibility for us. He is going to do everything He can to get us safely to the day of salvation without losing anyone. And along the way, He is going to make sure that we have everything we need, including divine health.

Look at the context of the above passage. It was right after Jesus fed the multitude. Why did He feed the multitude? He felt compassion for them. They had been there for several days, listening to His teachings, and were hungry. It was a long journey home without food and water. Jesus felt a responsibility for them. After all, they were in that situation because of Him. The disciples didn't have the money to buy enough food for everyone and only had five loaves of bread and a couple of fish. There was no way in the natural world that they were going to be fed. So, Jesus supernaturally intervened, and they were provided food. Jesus miraculously changed the composition of the bread and fish and multiplied them to meet the need.

There are dozens of instances when Jesus healed the sick and delivered those who were demon-possessed. God's heart has always been to provide healing for His children. If Jesus bore your sickness and diseases upon His body so that you might be physically healed at salvation, then wouldn't He also make a provision to heal you from our food supply that is making you sick?

Yes, He has! The provision is that you are to give thanks for our food before you eat it and you are to discern the body of Christ by taking the Lord's Supper with each meal. Then the food becomes blessed. Just like the manna from heaven brought health to the children of Israel, the Bread of Life will bring health to you. The children of Israel needed divine intervention because they didn't have any food. We have an abundance of food, but it's not healthy for us, and we're getting sick eating our food. Because our food is not perfectly healthy, we need divine intervention. Jesus is the divine intervention.

Friend, I didn't make the promises: God did. God said in His word that He was making a new covenant with us. God said that our sicknesses and diseases were put on Jesus. That is a better promise. If God provided healing for our sicknesses and diseases, wouldn't He also make a provision to make the food healthy so we wouldn't get sick in the first place? Manna from heaven and the Bread of Life are wondrous bread. What a provision God has made for us. He has done for us what He did for the children of Israel:

God healed them at the Lord's Passover; He saved them by the blood of the lamb on the door-post; He provided them manna from heaven to sustain them in the wilderness for forty years to get them to the Promised Land; and the result was abundant life and divine health.

Jesus took our sicknesses and diseases upon Himself on the cross. He wants to heal us at salvation; He saved us from our sins by His blood and gave us eternal life; He provides us with true manna from heaven through the partaking of the Lord's Supper; He sustains us until the last days; and the result is abundant life and divine health with better promises.

In the next chapter, you are going to see how you literally become "one flesh" with Christ through marriage when you partake of His body and blood.

CHAPTER 8
EAT, DRINK, AND BE MARRIED

And the two shall become one flesh. This is a great mystery, but I speak concerning Christ and the church. (Ephesians 5:31–32)

There are many wedding traditions and customs routinely practiced in the United States. There's the bouquet toss. Tradition says that the girl who catches it is the next person in line to be married. Women have been known to fight one another to snag the bouquet. There is also the garter toss. The man who catches it is also the next to be married. I don't think the guys are aware of that, or there would not be such a mad scramble for it. Garters are also a symbol of fertility. Catching it means you will have lots of children. Now, I know the single guys don't know that tradition!

There is the tradition of something old and something new. Something old symbolizes the bride's past, and something new symbolizes her future of prosperity and good fortune. There is something borrowed and something blue. Something borrowed stands for borrowed happiness, and something blue stands for purity, love, and fidelity.

It's bad luck to see the bride in her wedding dress before the wedding. That started many years ago because they were afraid if the groom saw the bride before the wedding, he might have second thoughts and run away. There is the unity candle that represents the two becoming one. We had that at our wedding. The wedding rings symbolize a circle with no end and there is no end to your love for each other.

Wedding cakes are not just for dessert. When the cake is cut, it's supposed to symbolize their first act together as a couple. Years ago, the wedding cake was crumbled on top of the wife's head. It was supposed to be a fertility aid. Now couples just smash it in each other's faces. I think it is to see who will get the upper hand in the marriage right away.

There are several bizarre wedding traditions and customs around the world. In China, the Tujia people prepare for a wedding by crying. The bride must cry for one hour a day for thirty straight days. Ten days into her crying, she is joined by her mother, and ten days after that, her grandmother. This continues until all females in the family cry one hour a day. The crying is not meant to be out of sadness but is an expression of joy and deep love.

In Sweden, the groom leaves the room, and the single men in the room get to kiss the bride. When they are done, the bride leaves the room and the single women get to kiss the groom. I'm not sure that's the best way to start a marriage. There are a lot of people at my wedding. I wouldn't want to kiss my wife. There were several people there I wouldn't want to kiss either. I think I would be more careful who I invited to the wedding if I knew I would have to kiss them!

In America, it's a tradition for the father of the bride to give her away, signifying his blessing on the marriage. In the Maasai tribe in Kenya, the father gives his blessing by spitting on his daughter's head and breasts. Spitting is supposed to bring good luck and good fortune. I don't know if I would want to kiss the bride right after her dad spit on her. On our wedding night, I would make sure the first thing she did was take a shower!

This is one tradition I am glad we have not adopted. In South Korea, the groom's friends remove his shoes and tie his feet together with a rope or sash. They then lift his legs off the ground and beat the soles of his feet with a stick. This is done to check the groom's strength and ability to endure pain. The thinking is if he can endure the beating, then he can endure anything his wife inflicts on him. In Scotland, the bride is pelted with trash and rotten vegetables, and spoiled milk is poured over her head. Same concept. If she can put up with that, she can handle living with her husband.

In Fiji, the groom is supposed to present a whale's tooth to the father of the bride. Not sure if he must get it directly from a whale or if he can just buy one at the local market. In Daur, China, a couple must dissect a chicken and cut out its liver. If the liver is healthy, they can set a date for their wedding. If not, then the wedding must be postponed. In Borneo, it's bad luck for either the bride or groom to use the bathroom on their wedding day until after the ceremony. I think I would plan a morning wedding.

At Greek weddings, the attendees pin money on the bride and groom. That's a good idea. I wish I had known about that tradition. We would have incorporated it into our wedding.

THE WEDDING CEREMONY IS MORE THAN SYMBOLISM

While there is much symbolism in the wedding ceremony, it is anything but symbolic to God and to the ones getting married. Webster's definition of a "ceremony" is "a formal religious or public occasion according to a traditional or prescribed form." A wedding is more than a formal ceremony to the bride and groom. It is personal. It is something the bride has looked forward to and planned for since she was a little girl.

I have heard some say it is just a piece of paper. Not to God. It is the moment when two individuals become one flesh. Here's what Jesus said about marriage:

> For this reason, a man shall leave his father and mother and be joined to his wife, and the two shall become one flesh; so, then

they are no longer two, but one flesh. (Mark 10:7)

How do two become one flesh? It's a spiritual mystery. You can certainly see how the act of intercourse is the joining of two into one, but it is more than a physical act. It's a spiritual union separate and distinct from any other relationship. Jesus said a man becomes "joined" to his wife. The Greek word for "joined" means yoked. The easiest way to understand that is to think of two oxen yoked together as a team. They literally cannot move unless they move together. They are inseparable. Conjoined twins are physically bound together in some way. They can't move apart from each other. They have two different minds, but their bodies are connected in a way that they are one. They cannot be separated without drastic surgery. A couple that is one flesh cannot be separated without a severe and destructive tearing apart of their spiritual oneness.

Another definition of "joined" is united. When a couple is married, they share everything. Or at least they should. A bride should have every benefit a groom can offer. All that is his becomes hers. I don't have a prenuptial agreement with my wife. Everything I have is hers, and everything she has is mine. I don't hold anything back from her, because I want our physical oneness to reflect our spiritual oneness.

YOU BECOME ONE FLESH WITH CHRIST AT SALVATION

But he who is joined to the Lord is one spirit with Him. (1 Corinthians 6:17)

The Bible says we are the bride of Christ (Ephesians 5:25–27). Jesus called Himself the bridegroom (Mark 2:19). There is rich symbolism in the Bible about the marriage of the Lamb and His bride, who is spotless and blameless. However, it's more than symbolism. Paul had a deep understanding of this concept and called it a mystery:

This is a great mystery, but I speak concerning Christ and the church. (Ephesians 5:32)

When Paul said that the two shall become one flesh, it was in the context of the marriage relationship, but he clarified and said he was revealing a deeper truth: the church is one flesh with Christ. Upon salvation, you become one flesh with Christ, not unlike the exclusive and unique relationship a married couple has with each other. Just as a couple forsakes all others and leaves their father and mother to cleave to each other in marriage, you do the same when you accept Christ as your Savior.

Just as a husband and wife become one flesh in marriage, signifying intimacy and oneness, your relationship with Christ is as intimate as the marriage relationship. It transcends all other relationships. You are exclusive to Christ. You forsake all others for Christ. The moment you invited Jesus Christ into your heart as your Lord and Savior, He became your groom. He became your exclusive life partner:

> Do you not know that your bodies are members of Christ? Shall I then take the members of Christ and make them members of a harlot? Certainly not! Or do you not know that he who is joined to a harlot is one body with her? For "the two," He says, "shall become one flesh." But he who is joined to the Lord is one spirit with Him. (1 Corinthians 6:15–17)

Our bodies are members of Christ. Just as a married man is unfaithful when he joins his body to another woman, we are like a harlot when we're unfaithful to Christ. In the Old Testament, God often called Israel a harlot who was being unfaithful to Him when they worshiped other gods and sacrificed to idols. God said He was a jealous God and demanded their faithfulness to Him. When you become one flesh with Christ, you are expected to be faithful to Him and Him alone just as a husband is to remain faithful to his wife.

And look at the benefits. Just as the groom gives all he has to his new wife; Christ has given us all He has. He doesn't hold anything back from us. Every eternal blessing is ours in Christ Jesus. What a beautiful picture of our relationship with Christ. Christ died on the cross as a sacrifice for our sins and then took us as His bride so we would be entitled to every spiritual blessing in the Heavenly places that belong to Him.

> Blessed be the God and Father of our Lord Jesus Christ, who has blessed us with every spiritual blessing in the heavenly places in Christ. (Ephesians 1: 3)

Here are the blessings found in Ephesians 1 that we have in the heavenly places in Christ because we are one flesh "in Him":

In Him, we have redemption through His blood (v. 7).

In Him, we have obtained an inheritance (v. 11).

In Him, we were sealed with the Holy Spirit of promise, who guarantees our inheritance will be there at the time of redemption (v. 13–14).

YOU REMAIN ONE FLESH WITH CHRIST THROUGH THE PARTAKING OF THE LORDS SUPPER

The Lord's Supper is representative of our oneness with Christ. The church has never fully understood or taught this truth. It is in the partaking of the Lord's Supper that we proclaim our oneness with Christ. We maintain our oneness with Christ by eating the bread and drinking the wine. Here is what Jesus said in John 6: 51-56 (NIV):

> I am the living bread that came down from heaven. Whoever eats this bread will live forever. This bread is my flesh, which I will give for the life of the world."

Then the Jews began to argue sharply among themselves, "How can this man give us his flesh to eat?"

Jesus said to them, "Very truly I tell you, unless you eat the flesh of the Son of Man and drink his blood, you have no life in you. Whoever eats my flesh and drinks my blood has eternal life, and I will raise them up at the last day. For my flesh is real food and my blood is real drink. Whoever eats my flesh and drinks my blood remains in me, and I in them.

Jesus said bread is His flesh and His flesh is what gives life to the world. Then He made a powerful statement: unless you eat the flesh of the Son of Man and drink of His blood, then you have no life in you. We have taken this verse as symbolic. "You have no life in you" doesn't sound symbolic to me. In fact, it sounds very serious. It sounds like a matter of life and death.

In verses fifty-five and fifty-six Jesus said His flesh was real food and that His blood was real drink. What did He mean by that? Was He just speaking metaphorically? Is this just symbolic, or is there something more to the body and blood of Christ? This is important to understand because He went on to say that when you eat His flesh and drink His blood, you "remain" in Him, and He remains in you.

The Jews had no understanding of what Jesus meant by eating His flesh. Not that you can really blame them. The pagans had a practice of eating the flesh and drinking the blood of sacrifices, even human sacrifices. God called that an abomination. They thought Jesus was crazy at best, heretical at worst, for saying someone should eat His flesh and blood.

Today, we've chosen to make this passage simply symbolic and, in the process, have lost much of its meaning. You need to understand this verse in relation to Jesus instituting the Lord's Supper. The verbiage is basically the same. In John 6, Jesus said you must eat of His flesh to have anything to do with Him. At the Lord's Supper, Jesus said the bread was His broken body and then gave it to His disciples to eat. In John, He said you must drink His blood to have life in you. At the Lord's Supper, He said the wine was His blood that was shed for their forgiveness of sins, and then He gave it to them to drink. In John 6, He told them they must eat and drink His flesh and blood, and at the Lord's Supper, He showed them how to do so. In John 6, He said real food and real drink were His flesh and blood, and at the Lord's Supper, He showed how bread and wine, which are real food and drink, can be eaten.

This passage in John 6 refers to our initial salvation. You cannot have eternal life without participating in the flesh and blood of Christ. Jesus literally took upon Himself, into His body, your sins, your sicknesses, and your pain and sorrows and you became one with Him in His death and in His resurrection. At salvation, you are one with Christ for an eternity. That will never change. The Lord's Supper is one of the main ways you maintain your closeness with Christ. John 6 says that whoever eats His flesh and drinks His blood "remains" in Him. The Lord's Supper is the primary way you remain in Him.

You become one flesh with Christ the moment of salvation, just as you become one flesh with your spouse the moment you are married and consummate that marriage. A couple remains one flesh by maintaining an ongoing sexual relationship. You remain one flesh with Christ by the ongoing participation of the Lord's Supper. The ongoing taking of His body and blood inside of you helps you to remain one flesh in Him. In other words, like a couple remains one flesh in the act of regular intercourse, when you partake of Christ's flesh and blood regularly, you continue your oneness with Him.

Jesus said if you don't eat His flesh and drink His blood, you have no life in you. The ongoing partaking of the Lord's Supper maintains the life of Christ in you. Taken literally, every time you take a meal, it should be the Lord's Supper for you. It is more than a ritual. It is as intimate as anything you do with Christ. Every bite of food is the bread of life, and you maintain Christ's body inside of you as you eat the bread that is His body. Every drink is the blood of Christ shed for the forgiveness of our sins. God said life is in the blood. You should discern by faith that the body and blood bring life inside of you every time you eat.

Think about that in the context of what Paul was saying about the Corinthians when he said they were weak, sick, and dying because they weren't discerning and honoring the body of Christ. When they were coming together to eat, they were indulging their flesh by overeating and getting drunk. They were making a mockery of the Lord's Supper. I think it was even more than that. The church of Corinth was acting like a harlot and not the bride of Christ.

We are acting like the harlot as well. We are allowing our love affair with food and drink to become more important than our love affair with Christ. That is why we are sick, weak, and dying prematurely just like the church of Corinth. They were under grace, just like we are under grace, but the grace did not profit them because it wasn't mixed with faith discerning what Christ said about His flesh and blood. We have made the Lord's Supper a ritual that is done occasionally, thinking that we are honoring the death of Christ. You can't expect to maintain closeness with your spouse if you are intimate three or four times a year any more than you can expect to remain close with Christ observing the Lord's Supper three or four times a year.

A married couple doesn't make love just once. The act of making love the first time is the consummation of becoming one flesh. They make love again and again because they are one flesh. You are the bride of Christ for the rest of your life. Even though you are married to Him only once, you need to maintain ongoing intimacy with Him as your husband. Every time you eat bread (food) and every time you drink wine (drink), you are reaffirming your love for Christ as His bride, taking His body and His blood symbolically and literally into your body, where it brings life. Just as the wife receives her husband into her body to remain one flesh with him, you receive the body and blood of Christ into your body so as to remain one flesh with Him as His bride.

One of the most powerful ways for you to see breakthroughs in your health is to see all food as the body of Christ and all drinks as the blood of Jesus and realize that, by eating and drinking, you are remaining one with Christ. Before I eat any meal, I first thank God for the food and receive it with thanksgiving as Jesus did, and then I take time to pause, reflect, and remember that the food is Christ's body and the drink is His blood. And I take the food and the drink with the expectation that it is bringing life to me, including healing, wellness, wholeness, and eternal life. My friend, this is an answer to your health problems.

JESUS DIET PRINCIPLE #5
Partaking of the Lord's Supper often, helps to maintain your closeness to Christ.

So, does that mean you can just eat anything you want anytime you want with no consequences? Can you eat a dozen donuts for breakfast every morning, and if you thank God for it, it won't hurt you? Can I have sex with any woman I want, anytime I want, and still maintain my close oneness with my wife? Of course not. Neither can you eat and drink anything you want without any regard for Christ and expect through your own self-effort to be healthy and an ideal weight. That's what the church of Corinth was doing. They were overeating and overdrinking. Paul didn't call them out for their gluttony and drunkenness. He called them out for not taking the body and blood of Christ seriously. For that matter, you can eat the healthiest meal you can find; if you aren't taking the body and blood of Christ into you, it will be of very little benefit to your health.

Churches today are not discerning properly the body of Christ. We have basically gone about eating whatever we want during the week without any real regard for Christ and the true meaning of the food and drink we consume. We might say a quick prayer beforehand, but then we just eat whatever we want never discerning we are one flesh with Christ through the eating of food and drink. We don't even place much importance on the act of the Lord's Supper when we do practice it. Most churches do the Lord's Supper a few times a year and think that is enough. No wonder we are weak, sick, and dying.

Don't misunderstand this principle. Once you believe in Christ and are saved, you are in Christ until the last day, sealed by the Holy Spirit. You do not remain saved by partaking of the Lord's Supper on an ongoing basis. It is one of the ways in which you maintain your intimacy with Christ. Just because you quit having sex with your wife doesn't mean you aren't married; it just means you lost your intimacy. Just because you aren't partaking of the Lord's Supper often doesn't mean you aren't still married to Christ; it just means you are not maintaining your intimacy and closeness.

It also means that you are not continually bringing His life into you. Jesus said if you don't eat His flesh and drink His blood, there is no life in you. There is life in us by the very fact that we did partake of His flesh and blood when we were saved. The Lord's Supper keeps that life flowing inside of you daily.

> "And it shall be, in that day,"
> Says the Lord,
> "That you will call Me 'My Husband,'
> And no longer call Me 'My Master,'"
> (Hosea 2:16)

In the old covenant, God was their Master. He was the judge of whether they were following the laws properly. In the new covenant, the Lord is no longer your Master, He is your Husband.

You have a new relationship with Him. It is a marriage that requires ongoing intimacy. In the next chapter, you are going to see all that your Husband has done for you.

CHAPTER 9
IT IS WHAT IT IS WAS

This chapter is radical. It may be the most important in this book. It is going to change your conception and perception of God forever. It's going to challenge what has been taught for years in our churches and is going to reveal something about our relationship with God that most people have never understood.

Congratulations for making it this far in this book. Most people don't make it past the first few chapters. Stephen Hawking did an unscientific study to determine how far people read in books. It's based on the number of underlines. He assumed that when the underlining stopped, then the person quit reading. He found that 43.4 percent of people finished Catching Fire from the Hunger Games Series, or at least kept underlining all the way through the last chapter. One of the classics, The Great Gatsby, was finished by 28.3 percent of the readers. Only 6.6 percent of the people finished Stephen Hawking's book A Brief History of Time. I wonder how he felt about his own study discovering that very few people thought his atheistic views of God and man were worth reading past a couple of chapters.

A little over twenty-five percent of people finished Fifty Shades of Grey. I wish it weren't that many. A whopping 98.5 percent finished The Goldfinch by Donna Tartt. I haven't read it, and I don't know what it's about, but it must be a compelling book that is hard to put down. Only 1.9 percent of the people finished Hillary Clinton's book Hard Choices. No surprise there. I'm not making a political statement; I just don't think it was the must-read of the year.

It is what it is. Most people start a book and don't finish it. It's hard to hold people's attention long enough for them to finish an entire book. I wonder who came up with the expression "It is what it is." You hear it all the time now. I find myself saying it more often than I wish. There are a number of expressions I heard growing up that I use more than I would like. I heard my parents and grandparents say things like, "He's as dumb as a rock," "He's as drunk as a skunk," "He's as strong as an ox," "He's lying like a dog," and "She's as pretty as a picture." I heard these a lot as well: "Money doesn't grow on trees," "Don't put all your eggs in one basket," and "The early bird gets the worm." It's funny how sayings catch on and become part of our vernacular.

There are a number of really strange sayings from around the world. One is "There is no cow on the ice." That means that there's no reason to worry. Another similar saying by the Polish is "Not my circus. Not my monkeys." That means it's not my problem. It's like our saying "No skin off my back." When someone says you are "pretending to be an Englishman," it means you are pretending to be innocent when you really aren't. That sounds like a slight to English men. They should be offended by that statement and probably are.

"To set the dogs on someone" in Latin America means to flirt with someone. The Portuguese say, "Don't feed the donkey the sponge cake." That means don't waste your time or money on someone who doesn't deserve it or need it. You've probably heard our saying "Happy as a pig in slop." The Germans say something similar: "Live like a maggot in bacon." I like our saying better. The Russians have a saying, "I'm not hanging noodles on your ears." That means they are telling the truth. To give someone a pumpkin in Spain means you stood them up for a date.

Teenagers today have adopted strange sayings and turned them into mainstream expressions to the detriment of our society.

"Killing it" actually means you are doing something really good. When a kid says, "That is bad," sometimes, he's saying that it's good. It must be confusing for parents these days. When you tell their kids they are bad, they say, "Thank you!" When kids say they are "mad," it means they think something is awesome. What do they say when they are really mad? Do they still say they're mad? How do you tell the difference? Not sure you can tell from their body language. They always seem mad to me even when they are happy.

And kids these days are getting extremely annoying. I hope their use of "like" and "right" after every other word is only a phase they will grow out of soon. I mean it is, like, really annoying, when, like, I'm having a conversation with a teenager, and he, like, says like over and over again. That drives me, like, crazy! Am I right?

I guess our phrases when we were growing up weren't much better. "It's as cold as hell" is really a stupid thing to say. Everything I've read about hell is that it's very hot. It's not cold at all. Where did we come up with something that's so inaccurate? Why do we say something over and over again when the opposite of what we're saying is really the truth? Have you ever heard the phrase "Break a leg?" That doesn't sound like something nice to say to someone. It actually means good luck. It stems from an old superstition that if you wish evil on someone, then you are actually wishing them good luck. It's a strange way to wish someone luck. I would never want to wish evil on someone.

Did you know that Jesus actually used opposite things to illustrate His points? Jesus said, "Give and it shall be given unto you." The whole concept of giving money in the Bible is a counterintuitive principle. If you give away your money, you'll have more money later than you had when you started. If you hold on to your money tightly, then you'll have less money than you would have if you had given it away. That doesn't seem logical. It doesn't make much sense to the world.

Did you know that the right side of your brain controls the left side of your body and vice versa? God created us that way. I'm sure you have heard the term "Opposites attract." That's true. It seems like the most successful married couples are those in which the two are complete opposites of each other. God designed it that way. They are one flesh. Two opposites create more of a whole person. His strengths are usually her weaknesses. Her strengths usually complement his weaknesses. They are better together than they are apart because they each have opposite attributes that help the other.

"It is what it is" is another phrase that God does not agree with. The Bible says that faith is the substance of things not seen. Romans 4:17 says God calls those things that do not exist as though they did. You're not to live your life accepting things as they appear. You are to live your life based on what God has said is true, not necessarily on what seems to be true in the natural world. That is counterintuitive.

Read what happened when Jesus met the Royal official whose son was near death:

> Once more he visited Cana in Galilee, where he had turned the water into wine. And there was a certain royal official whose son lay sick at Capernaum. When this man heard that Jesus had arrived in Galilee from Judea, he went to him and begged him to come and heal his son, who was close to death.
>
> "Unless you people see signs and wonders," Jesus told him, "you will never believe."
>
> The royal official said, "Sir, come down before my child dies."
>
> "Go," Jesus replied, "your son will live."
>
> The man took Jesus at his word and departed. While he was still on the way, his servants met him with the news that his boy was living. When he inquired as to the time when his son got better,

they said to him, "Yesterday, at one in the afternoon, the fever left him."

Then the father realized that this was the exact time at which Jesus had said to him, "Your son will live." So, he and his whole household believed. (John 4:46-53 NIV)

The royal official came to Jesus and begged him to heal his son. That's not the way to get God to heal you. Begging doesn't work. Begging is an outward expression of doubt. It's not enough to believe that God can heal you; there has to be the faith that He is going to heal you. Jesus even admonished him saying, "Will you not believe unless you see a sign?" Then the man's faith arises within him. Jesus spoke the words, "Your son will live." I love what this verse says next: "The man took Jesus at His word and departed." What a tremendous expression of faith! "I don't need to see that my son lives. I believe what Jesus said is true. If he said my son lives, then I believe it." And he put action to his faith and departed believing that his son was going to be alright.

On the way home, I wonder if the man had any doubts. It would be perfectly normal for him to say, "I'll believe it when I see it." On the way home, a servant met him to give him the good news that his son was better. Turns out his son had been healed at the exact moment Jesus had said he was healed! Then his entire family was saved. And why wouldn't they have been? They had just seen a tremendous sign and wonder. When there was no hope for their son, Jesus healed him without even coming to their house. Jesus just spoke the words, "Your son will live," and a miracle happened. And the man believed it even though he didn't see it.

"It is what it is" is not always a true statement. It is whatever God says it is. Jesus said, "Blessed are those who have not seen and yet believe." The best expression of faith is believing what you don't see in the natural world, especially if it is actually the opposite of what you see.

I'm going to share with you now a revelation from Scripture that I only recently learned. Faith is not just believing that God is going to do something in the future; faith is actually believing God has already done it in the past. This came to me when I realized that almost all the promises in the new covenant are in the past tense. This is what it says in Ephesians 1:3:

> Blessed be the God and Father of our Lord Jesus Christ, who has blessed us with every spiritual blessing in the heavenly places in Christ,

"Blessed us" is past tense. It means God has already done it. He has already blessed us with every spiritual blessing in the heavenly places in Christ. Read what it says about healing in 1 Peter 2:24:

> Who Himself bore our sins in His own body on the tree, that we, having died to sins, might live for righteousness—by whose stripes you **were** healed. (Emphasis Added)

By His stripes, we "were" healed. That is past tense. If we were healed, that means we are already healed. Here is what it says in Isaiah 53:5:

> But He was wounded for our transgressions,
> He was bruised for our iniquities;
> The chastisement for our peace was upon Him,
> And by His stripes we are healed.

Do you see the difference in tenses? Isaiah was written before Jesus died. It says that "we are healed." In other words, we will be healed. Jesus had not yet come to be the sacrifice for our healing. He had not yet taken the stripes. After He took the stripes, the Bible changed tenses. Now we were healed, past tense. It has already happened. We are not going to be healed in the future. We were already healed in our past. Our sicknesses and diseases were put upon Jesus on the cross.

Here is what the Bible says that Jesus did for us in the past tense:

> He himself bore our sins" in his body on the cross, so that we might die to sins and live for righteousness. (1 Peter 2:24)

> He Himself took our infirmities and bore our sicknesses. (Matthew 8:17)

> Surely, he took up our pain and bore our suffering. (Isaiah 53:4 NIV)

Jesus bore (past tense) our sins, bore our sicknesses, and bore our sorrows. The Greek word for "bore" means carried or took upon Himself. If my wife was carrying a suitcase and I took it from her and carried it myself, I bore the burden of carrying the suitcase. Jesus took upon Himself our sins, sicknesses, and sorrows and carried them so that we don't have to. Here is what we have to realize: He has already done it.

In John 19:30, right before Jesus died, He cried out, "It is finished." What was finished? What Jesus did for us in the new covenant. Forgiveness of sin was finished. Healing of sickness and disease was finished. Our burden of carrying sorrows was finished. The work was completely done once and for all. There was nothing left to do.

If you're sick, you don't have to believe God is going to heal you sometime in the future; you need to believe that God has already provided the provision for healing in the past. That is counterintuitive. That is the opposite of what seems normal and natural. That is hard to believe. When you're taking the Lord's Supper with every meal, you need to do so by taking God at His word, believing it and proclaiming that God has already healed you.

I know. That's hard to believe. In fact, many critics are going to read what I'm saying and dismiss it as totally misguided, and even heresy. Most people have a hard time believing we are supposed to act like God has already healed us. Most people approach it this way: "I know God can heal me if He wants to. I just don't know if

He will." You will likely never receive anything from God if that is what you believe.

You have to believe that you have already received your healing. Before you reject that statement, read what Jesus said about prayer and faith:

Therefore, I tell you, whatever you ask for in prayer, believe that you **have** received it, and it will be yours. (Mark 1:24 NIV) (Emphasis Added)

Believe you have already received it! Your prayers should be in past tense. Not that you are going to receive it. Not that you are begging God to do it. Not that someday, if the Lord is willing and the creek don't rise, you will receive your healing. You have to believe you have already received it. And that makes sense. If by His stripes we were healed, then we were healed. If we were healed, then we are healed. I pray this prayer and say this confession all the time:

If I were healed, that means I am healed. If I am healed, then this sickness has no right to be in my body. I am already healed in the name of Jesus by His work on the cross."

When I'm getting ready to eat my meal, I thank God for what He has already done for me. I'm not asking God to do something in the future; I'm thanking Him for what He's already done in the past.

Let me explain it this way. If my car breaks down and I take it to the shop and they fix it, the car has been healed in a way. Whatever was wrong with it is fixed. The shop calls me and tells me it is fixed. It doesn't really matter if I believe them or not; the car is already fixed. I haven't seen with my own eyes that it's fixed, but I choose to believe that it is because of what they told me. At some point, I'll see it with my own eyes and will realize firsthand that the car is working fine, but in the meantime, I just believe what I was told that the car is fixed.

In a similar way, God has told us that He has made a provision for our sins, sicknesses, and sorrows. That provision is Christ on the cross. They are called the finished works of Christ, meaning they are already done. God has already forgiven you of all your sins, past, present, and future. You may be thinking, "How could God forgive my sins I haven't yet committed?" You may be having a hard time believing that God has already forgiven your future sins. You had better hope He has forgiven you of future sins. Every sin you ever committed was in the future at the time Christ died. Only God could know every sin you would ever commit and place them on Jesus two thousand years before you ever committed them.

Only God could know every sickness and disease that would enter your body years after Christ and go ahead and make provision for them. Only God could know every pain and every sorrow and let Jesus bear them on the cross on your behalf. All you have to do is recognize it's already done and thank God for it.

Just like the royal official, we should just take Jesus at His word. He said, "This is my body that is broken for you. Do this in remembrance of me." In other passages, Scripture says His body was broken for our sicknesses. Jesus said that as often as you eat and drink, do this in remembrance of Him. Every time you eat anything, remember the broken body of Jesus. Every time you sit down to partake of a meal, receive the meal with thanksgiving and rejoice that your sins are already forgiven, and your sicknesses are already healed.

And don't doubt. Read James 1:6–7 (NIV):

But when you ask, you must believe and not doubt, because the one who doubts is like a wave of the sea, blown and tossed by the wind. That person should not expect to receive anything from the Lord.

Let's put this passage together with what Jesus said in Mark 11:24. James said that when you ask, you must believe and not doubt. What is it you are to believe and not doubt? Jesus said you are to believe and not doubt that you have already received what you are asking for! If you doubt, what is the result? That person should not expect to receive anything from the Lord.

That is the essence of the new covenant. It's always accessed by faith. We no longer have to keep a set of rules and laws. We just have to believe without doubt. What do you have to believe without doubt? That your sins are already forgiven. Jesus bore those on the cross. You're already healed from your sicknesses and diseases because Jesus bore those when He took the stripes upon His back. You have to believe that your pain and sorrows were carried by Jesus on the cross. You have to believe, without doubt, that you have already received these things. If you have already received them, then your prayers should be of thanksgiving, thanking God for what He has already done for you.

That's why we are weak, sick, and dying prematurely. We are not discerning the body of Christ. We have not recognized that Jesus has already done everything He is going to do for us on this earth. God has already made every provision for you that He is ever going to make on this earth until you get to Heaven, where Jesus is preparing a place for you right now.

That is why the prayer of thanksgiving before every meal is so important. That's why the Lord's Supper has so much power in our lives. Christ has done so much for us. He bore so much and took so much of our sins, sicknesses, and sorrows upon Himself. He carried them all, suffering tremendous pain and agony on our behalf, so much so that He cried out to God, "Why have you forsaken me?" Jesus was forsaken by His Father so we could be embraced by God the Father. He became our sin so we could become the righteousness of God in Christ. He took our sicknesses upon Himself so that we wouldn't have to suffer with them. He took our sorrows so we wouldn't have to live in constant heartache.

"It is what it is" is not applicable to us today when it comes to God. It is what it was. You don't have to accept what is if it contradicts what God says it was. You don't have to accept what you see in the natural world if it contradicts what Christ said He did for you on the cross. When God gives you a promise in the past tense, you accept it and appropriate it by faith.

Years ago, Abraham Lincoln signed the Emancipation Proclamation. He signed a document giving freedom to all slaves. Were all slaves immediately free? Yes and no. Many still faced years of pain, bondage, and hardship. Legally, they were free, but they had to be liberated from their bondage. They had to be delivered from their captivity. If a slave didn't know about the Emancipation Proclamation, he would keep living like a slave. If he knew about it but didn't believe it, he would keep living like a slave.

In a similar way, God has declared you free. Free from sin, sickness, bondage, pain, and sorrows. You just need to see the manifestation of it. If you don't know that you have already been set free, you will keep living like you weren't. If you know but you don't believe it, then you will keep living in bondage. If you didn't know that you were free before, you know now. There is no excuse. You are free! You have been emancipated.

> It is for freedom that Christ has set us free. Stand firm, then, and do not let yourselves be burdened again by a yoke of slavery. (Galatians 5:1 NIV)

Don't let yourself be burdened again with a yoke of slavery. You were (past tense) set free whether you live like it or not.

> So if the Son sets you free, you will be free indeed. (John 8:36 NIV)

That is how God has interacted with His children throughout the centuries. He told Noah to build an ark because a flood was coming. He told Moses He was leading them to a Promised Land that would be theirs. He told Joshua that He had given Jericho into his hands:

> Then the Lord said to Joshua, "See, I have delivered Jericho into your hands, along with its king and its fighting men. March

around the city once with all the armed men. Do this for six days. (Joshua 6:2–3 NIV)

God said that He had already delivered (past tense) Jericho into their hands. What they did would be in the future: march around the city for six days. God's work was in the past tense; their work was in the future tense. That's how God does things. He does the work first, and then, if we believe it, we will follow the instructions, and what God promised will come to pass.

That is how it is with our healing. God already did the work through Christ. What we do is now and in the future. Our actions determine whether it is manifested or not. If Joshua doesn't march around Jericho for six days, the city will not be delivered into his hands no matter how much he begs God. If you don't thank God for your food before you eat it, the food is not consecrated. If you don't discern the body of Christ before you eat your food and drink your beverages, then you will not receive the manifestation of the bread of life into your body. It doesn't change the fact that Christ died on the cross. It doesn't change the fact that those things are already promised to you by God. It just means that you won't see it manifested.

Begging God is not going to make any difference. God doesn't generally respond to our needs. He responds to our faith. We think that just because we are suffering and need healing, God should go ahead and heal us. It doesn't work that way in the new covenant. You have to believe that God has already done it for you. You have to believe you have already received it. Today, you don't have to march around Jericho for six days. That was the old covenant. They had to obey God in order to see the promises fulfilled. All we have to do is believe God, and the promises are ours.

Time, then, is the proof of our faith. Hebrews 10: 35–36 says:

Therefore do not cast away your confidence, which has great reward. For you have need of endurance, so that after you have done the will of God, you may receive the promise

Keep your confidence and you will see the reward. You need endurance so you have the patience to wait to receive the promise. The promise is past tense. The reward is manifested today or in the future. Your faith, confidence, and endurance will lead you to the manifestation.

Don't be discouraged if you don't see immediate results with the Jesus Diet. Some of you may see instantaneous results. I hope you do. Others will see the manifestation over time. Maintain your confidence. Keep thanking God for your food and keep partaking of the Lord's Supper, honoring the body of Christ, with each meal. You will see the reward. You have to because the hard work is already done by God through Christ. It is what it was!

CHAPTER 10
SICK OF BEING SICK

For the message of the cross is foolishness to those who are perishing, but to us who are being saved it is the power of God.
(1 Corinthians 1:18)

Through the years, humans have obsessively sought cures for all manner of sicknesses and disease. Some people touting the cures have been well meaning and others have simply been charlatans trying to scam desperate victims. With the ability of hindsight, we can see how foolish many of their supposed cures were.

For instance, in ancient Egypt, physicians used dead mice as a cure for toothaches. A mouse was mashed into a paste and placed on the tooth. This treatment would supposedly relieve pain and inflammation. As late as the 1800s, mice paste was used as a treatment for small-pox, measles, whooping cough, and bed-wetting. It supposedly worked. I think if someone told me they were going to put dead mouse mash on me, I would be cured pretty fast, too!

Before it was known that arsenic was a deadly poison, it was widely used as medicine. The Chinese thought it cured malaria. Even as late as the 1950s, it was used to treat arthritis and diabetes. Victorian women even used it in their cosmetics, not realizing the poison was entering their bloodstream through their skin. I can't "make-up" these things (pun intended).

Have you ever heard the term "snake oil salesman"? They actually existed. For years, it was believed snake oil relieved joint pain, and actual salesmen shamelessly hawked various formulas to unsuspecting victims who were instructed to rub the oil on to painful areas. Of course, the oil didn't work, and eventually, they figured out it was a scam, and that is where the term comes from.

Some home remedies were so outrageous it's hard to believe anyone ever tried them. Years ago, dog poop was a home remedy for sore throats. I would rather have a sore throat. Crocodile dung was used as a common contraceptive by ancient Egyptians. I'm not going to describe how it was used. You can look it up for yourself. Over the years, tree sap, lemon halves, cotton wool, and elephant dung have been used for the same purpose.

In the 1800s, heroin was widely used for coughs, colds, and pain. I can see how that might make you feel better temporarily. In 1849, two druggists from Bangor, Maine, developed a formula for infants who were teething. It was marketed as Mrs. Winslow's Soothing Syrup. More than 1.5 million bottles were sold. It definitely relieved the infant's pain and calmed them down. The two main ingredients were morphine and alcohol! The American Medical Association denounced the product in 1911, but it continued to be sold until 1930.

When cigarettes first came on the scene, they were touted as a cure for cancer. I'm not kidding. Moldy bread was commonly used as a disinfectant for cuts. There was some basis to believe it had some medicinal value; it eventually led to the discovery of penicillin which comes from mold.

In 1863, an Italian chemist developed a tonic of coca leaves treated with red wine. The coca leaves contained cocaine and those who drank the concoction felt much better afterward. Thomas Edison, Queen Victoria, the czar of Russia, and many other famous people swore by the product. John S. Pemberton developed a similar formula in the United States that sold very well under the brand name Coca-Cola.

Some of the treatments bordered on the barbaric. In the eighteenth and nineteenth centuries, a procedure called hemiglossectomy was developed for stuttering. The surgeon cut off half of the patient's tongue! That was before anesthesia, so the procedure was extremely painful and many of the patients bled to death.

Dr. Benjamin Rush was a signer of the Declaration of Independence and was thought to be the greatest physician of his day. He believed pain was the cure for most diseases, including mental illness. He cut patients with knives, bound their hands and feet, essentially cutting off circulation, doused them with cold water for hours on end, and poured acid on their backs. He believed pain permanently discharged mental illness from their brains. He developed what was called the gyrator, which hung patients from ropes, where they were spun in circles for hours. He believed the spinning increased circulation to the point to where the disease would leave the body.

Leech therapy dates all the way back to the pyramids. Also, commonly known as "blood-letting," leeches were used to treat everything from headaches to hemorrhoids. In the 1800s, more than forty million leeches a year were harvested and sold for medicinal purposes in France alone. They weren't just used externally. In one procedure, a leech was attached to a string and lowered down the patient's throat and into the stomach. Sometimes the strings broke, and the leech was lost inside the victim. It is said that leech therapy is making a comeback. Apparently, a well-known actress swears by it and uses leeches to maintain her youthful appearance.

Trepanation dates back seven thousand years but was used as recently as the late 1800s as a treatment for headaches. The procedure involved drilling a hole in the patient's skull. It was believed it would relieve the pressure in the skull and cure the headaches. I'm guessing women didn't claim to have a headache in the 1800s as much as they do now.

One such treatment is better known today as a lobotomy and in the twentieth century, it was used for all types of medical issues, especially mental disorders. More than forty thousand lobotomies were performed on patients in the 1900s. Today, it is considered butchery, but at the time, it was lauded by the New York Times as "the surgery for the soul." The developer of the process actually won the Nobel Prize in medicine. Looking for a safer option, a procedure known as the "ice pick lobotomy" became standard protocol. An ice pick was hammered through the orbit of the eye below the eyelid. It was used on patients as young as four years old! It was better than drilling a hole in a person's head, and the developer defended the practice all the way to his grave, but it is universally regarded as a dark age in medicine and is known now as "the worst idea of the mind."

Do you realize that future generations are going to look back at many of our current medical procedures with the same disbelief? Some of our treatments today may someday be regarded as barbaric as lobotomies. It's not that doctors and researchers are not well-meaning; it's just that they have limited knowledge. What seems like a good idea now, may be considered foolish years later, when more information is available. However, it won't matter how many advances in science we make in the coming years; doctors will never replace the healing power of God in our lives. Read the account of the woman with the issue of blood in Mark 5:25–34:

> Now a certain woman had a flow of blood for twelve years and had suffered many things from many physicians. She had spent all that she had and was no better, but rather grew worse. When she heard about Jesus, she came behind Him in the crowd and touched His garment. For she said, "If only I may touch His clothes, I shall be made well.
>
> Immediately the fountain of her blood was dried up, and she felt in her body that she was healed of the ¹affliction. And Jesus, immediately knowing in Himself that power had gone out of Him,

turned around in the crowd and said, "Who touched My clothes?"

But His disciples said to Him, "You see the multitude thronging You, and You say, 'Who touched Me?'"

And He looked around to see her who had done this thing. But the woman, fearing and trembling, knowing what had happened to her, came and fell down before Him and told Him the whole truth.

And He said to her, "Daughter, your faith has made you well. Go in peace and be healed of your affliction."

The woman spent all she had on doctors and was worse. Not that she had any alternative other than to turn to doctors; she had been bleeding for twelve years. Here, are some of the symptoms of a blood disorder:

Deep internal bleeding. Bleeding occurs in deep muscle causing limbs to swell. The swelling presses on nerves and leads to numbness and pain.

Damage to joints. Internal bleeding puts pressure on joints causing severe pain. Frequent internal bleeding leads to arthritis and destruction of joints.

Infection. The blood disorder weakens the immune system making the person more susceptible to colds, flus, viruses and infections.

Adverse reaction to blood clotting. The immune system reacts to clotting and develops proteins that try to activate clotting. Over time, when it is unsuccessful, it eventually develops proteins that inactivate clotting.

The woman was in tremendous pain and likely all alone. Her husband and family had probably abandoned her because she was considered unclean by Jewish law. She wasn't allowed to touch anyone or be touched. She could have been stoned to death just for touching Jesus's garment. She wasn't allowed to worship at the Temple, so she might have even felt cut off from God. We know she was poor because these verses say she had "spent all she had."

But then she "heard about Jesus." I love that verse. Have you heard about Jesus? Have you heard about how Jesus heals the sick? Jesus did what the doctors could not do, and He healed her immediately of the condition. In fact, He didn't really heal her; she took her healing from Him. She didn't ask permission to be healed. Jesus didn't ask her questions to ascertain if she had enough faith to be healed. She just believed she would be healed if she touched His garment, and she pushed through the crowd, touched His garment, and was healed.

Jesus was the best alternative to doctors then and is the best alternative to doctors today. Please don't take that the wrong way. Doctors are an incredible gift from God. Medical breakthroughs have been amazing and continue to be used by God to bring healing to millions. I have no doubt today's doctors would have much more success in treating the woman with the issue of blood than the doctors of her day. One hundred years from now, doctors will likely be even better. Prescription drugs have eradicated many diseases and have eased human suffering. However, did you know that more people die today from prescription drug overdoses than illegal drugs? Medical mistakes are the leading cause of death in America. Our doctors and pharmacists are far from infallible and cannot be counted on to get everything right.

For instance, up until the mid-1800s, doctors performed autopsies and then delivered babies without washing their hands. Many mothers and their babies died during delivery. A physician in 1846 finally made the connection and began requiring his staff to wash their hands with a disinfectant after handling a corpse. All they had to do was read the Bible. God told the children of Israel in Numbers 19:11 that anyone who touched a dead body was unclean for seven days and must be separated from the rest of the population.

That is exactly my point: my faith is in God, not in doctors. Even if I need to go to a doctor, I trust God for my healing and not the doctor. God may use the doctor, but I still consider Him my source. I'm also convinced that following the Jesus Diet will resolve many sicknesses and diseases and make doctors less necessary for Christians.

There are three truths you must understand in order to see the manifestation of healing in your life:

1. It is God's will for His children to be healed physically as well as spiritually.
2. God is not a respecter of persons. Every promise in the new covenant is equally available to every believer.
3. Jesus provided healing on the cross. We access that healing through faith.

GOD'S WILL IS FOR HIS CHILDREN TO BE HEALED

I'm not sure why most people still don't believe this truth. You have to basically ignore the Scriptures in order to conclude that God doesn't want us to be healthy and healed of our sicknesses and diseases. It has been His will since the beginning of time. Look at the following old covenant verses to understand the heart of God when it comes to sickness and disease:

> If you diligently heed the voice of the LORD your God and do what is right in His sight, give ear to His commandments and keep all His statutes, I will put none of the diseases on you which I have brought on the Egyptians. For I am the LORD who heals you. (Exodus 15:26)

> O Lord my God, I cried out to You, and You healed me. (Psalms 30:2)

And forget not all His benefits; Who forgives all your iniquities, Who heals all your diseases. (Psalm 103:2-3)

He sent His word and healed them and delivered them from their destructions. (Psalm 107:20)

He heals the brokenhearted and binds up their wounds. (Psalm 147:3)

My son, give attention to my words; incline your ears to my sayings. Do not let them depart from your eyes; Keep them in the midst of your heart; For they are life to those who find them, and health to all their flesh. (Proverbs 4:20–22)

Then your light shall break forth like the morning, your healing shall spring forth speedily, and your righteousness shall go before you; The glory of the LORD shall be your rear guard. (Isaiah 58:8)

Return, you backsliding children, And I will heal your backslidings. Indeed, we do come to You, For You are the LORD our God. (Jeremiah 3:22)

Heal me, O LORD, and I shall be healed; Save me, and I shall be saved, For You are my praise. (Jeremiah 17:14)

For I will restore health to you and heal you of your wounds, says the LORD, Because they called you an outcast saying: "This is Zion; No one seeks her." (Jeremiah 30:17)

Behold, I will bring it health and healing; I will heal them and reveal to them the abundance of peace and truth. (Jeremiah 33:6)

Come and let us return to the LORD; For He has torn, but He will heal us; He has stricken, but He will bind us up. (Hosea 6:1)

Jesus said He came to do the will of the Father (John 6:38). He said He doesn't do anything except what the Father tells Him to do. With that clarity, Jesus said He came for those who are sick:

When Jesus heard it, He said to them, "Those who are well have no need of a physician, but those who are sick. I did not come to call the righteous, but sinners, to repentance." (Mark 2:17)

JESUS DIET PRINCIPLE #6
Jesus came to provide spiritual and physical healing.

How could God's will be anything but healing since it was such a big part of Jesus's ministry? The above verse has mostly been interpreted with a spiritual application. Jesus clearly was talking about healing our spiritual sickness caused by sin. However, if Jesus was only interested in spiritual healing, why was healing physical sicknesses such a priority in His ministry? There was never a single instance in the Bible when Jesus did not heal someone who asked for healing.

GOD IS NOT A RESPECTER OF PERSONS

Read Acts 10:34:

Then Peter opened his mouth and said, "In truth I perceive that God shows no partiality."

Peter said, "in truth" meaning this is a truth we need to know. What is the truth that is so important for us to know? That God does not show partiality. Another translation says God shows no favoritism. Every promise of the old covenant was available to every Jewish person if they followed the instructions. Every promise in the new covenant is available to everyone, including unbelievers:

He is the atoning sacrifice for our sins, and not only for ours but also for the sins of the whole world. (1 John 2:2 NIV)

Jesus died for the sins of the whole world. Does that mean that all people are saved? Not everyone is saved because not everyone believes. That doesn't mean salvation is not available to them; they just don't receive it.

> Beloved, I wish above all things that thou mayest prosper and be in health, even as thy soul prospereth. (3 John 2:2 KJV)

God wishes above all things that we prosper and be in health just as our soul prospers since we are saved for an eternity. God's heartfelt desire is that everyone is in good health. Does that mean that everyone is healed? Not everyone is healed, just like not everyone is saved, because not all people receive healing. That doesn't mean it's not available to everyone just that not everyone receives it.

More to the point, God would not make healing available to one person and not to another. He's no respecter of persons. You can be male or female, black or white, rich or poor, educated or uneducated, or fit any other category, and it is not in God's nature to discriminate against you.

If God healed the woman with the issue of blood, then this verse would not be true if He wouldn't do the same thing for you. If God healed the blind man or the paralytic, He would not be a good God if He wouldn't do it for you as well. If Paul can eat unclean foods by just saying a prayer of thanksgiving, then you can too.

WE ACCESS HEALING BY FAITH

God is not withholding anything from you:

> The Lord will give grace and glory;
> No good thing will He withhold
> From those who walk uprightly.
> (Psalm 84:11)

God does not withhold any good thing to those who walk uprightly. That is old covenant terminology, meaning that God did withhold good things from those who didn't walk uprightly. In the new covenant God does not withhold any good thing from those who believe in Jesus and access grace by faith. Notice it says that the Lord will give grace and glory. That is a prophecy of something to come. Jesus is the Lord and He came to give grace and glory to you and me. We access that grace by faith.

> For by grace you have been saved through faith, and that not of yourselves; it is the gift of God. (Ephesians 2:8)

The word *salvation* in this verse is the Greek word "sozo," which means wholeness. That verse is not just talking about salvation from sins, although that's part of it. It's also talking about health and wellness, which is a part of wholeness. You cannot separate out the works of Christ. You don't pick and choose which parts of salvation are available to you. They're all available and are free gifts of grace.

You can certainly choose to be saved from your sins and not healed of your sicknesses, but that is your choice, not God's. You will discover in the Jesus Diet that many of your sicknesses and diseases will go away from the eating of your food with thanksgiving and the honoring of the body of Christ through the Lord's Supper. If you don't see immediate results, you will over time.

Beyond that, you need to rely on Jesus to give the Holy Spirit instructions on what you need to do to see the manifestation of healing. He may tell you to go to a doctor. He may tell you to take a certain medication or supplement. Whatever He tells you to do, do it. If the Holy Spirit is telling you not to follow the doctor's advice, then don't. Just wake up every day believing that God wants you well, and you will be.

ONE WORD CAN MAKE ALL THE DIFFERENCE

In the structure of a sentence, one word and even one comma can make all the difference in its meaning. If you say, "Let's eat, Dad," it means you're telling your dad you are ready to eat. If you say, "Let's eat Dad," it means you want to eat your dad for dinner. If you say, "Let's eat a pizza," you are talking in general terms, which could mean you still need to order the pizza. If you say, "Let's eat the pizza," you are talking about a specific pizza that you probably already have. The meaning of a sentence is dramatically changed if you use "the" instead of "a."

There are two passages that can be interpreted in two different ways based on whether "a" is used or "the" is used in the translation. Read 1 Corinthians 10:12–17:

> Therefore let him who thinks he stands take heed lest he fall. No temptation has overtaken you except such as is common to man; but God is faithful, who will not allow you to be tempted beyond what you are able, but with the temptation will also make **the way of escape**, that you may be able to bear it. Therefore, my beloved, flee from idolatry. I speak as to wise men; judge for yourselves what I say. The cup of blessing which we bless, is it not the communion of the blood of Christ? The bread which we break, is it not the communion of the body of Christ? For we, though many, are one bread and one body; for we all partake of that one bread. (1 Corinthians 10:12–17) (Emphasis Added)

In verse thirteen, the word "temptation" means trial. It is not just temptation to sin but includes any trial you may encounter, including sickness. Verse thirteen is a passage whose meaning can change based on using "the" instead of "a." Notice the difference in the meaning of the sentence if one word is changed:

> ... but with the temptation will always make "a" way of escape (emphasis added).

> ... but with the temptation will always make "the" way of escape (emphasis added).

I have seen verse thirteen translated both ways. If "a" is used, it means that there are many ways of escape, and you must find which one to use. "If "the" is used, it means there is one way of escape, and you need to know what it is, and if you will use that way, then you will escape. It should be translated "the way of escape," which is how it is translated in the New King James Version. The next two verses tell us "the way of escape." It is to flee from idolatry and remember the meaning of the Lord's Supper. Idolatry is putting anything else above God, and the Lord's Supper is putting God first.

Let's look at another passage in which the same translation applies:

> For I say, through the grace given unto me, to every man that is among you, not to think of himself more highly than he ought to think; but to think soberly, according as God hath dealt to every man **the measure of faith**.
>
> For as we have many members in one body, and all members have not the same office: So we, being many, are one body in Christ, and everyone members one of another. (Romans 12:3-5 KJV) (Emphasis Added)

Verse three says that God has given every man faith. The meaning of the verse changes if "the" is used instead of "a."

God hath dealt to every man "a" measure of faith (emphasis added).

God hath dealt to every man "the" measure of faith (emphasis added).

The New King James Version uses "a," and the original King James Version uses "the." The meaning is totally different based on which word is used. "A measure of faith" could mean that God gives each person a different amount of faith. "The measure of faith" means that God gives the same amount to everyone. Scripture passages should be interpreted with other passages. In that God is no respecter of persons, "the measure of faith" is the best translation because it reinforces the belief that God treats all of us the same. This is particularly important as it relates to healing because many think the reason they are not healed is that they don't have enough faith.

If God has given everyone the same measure of faith, then you have all the faith you need to be healed. Your faith is no different from Paul's faith other than that he might have used his faith more effectively than you do. Notice in this passage of scripture that Paul also references the Lord's Supper when he says we are "one body in Christ." He used the same terminology in 1 Corinthians 10 when he talked about the way of escape that he used in Romans 12 when he talked about the measure of faith given to every man. Put these two verses together, and you find the power of the Lord's Supper. The body and blood of Christ is the way of escape from your trials, including the trial of sickness and disease. You have been given all the faith you need to escape your trial by being in Christ. God gave you that faith by grace because you are in Christ.

If you are sick, the ultimate way of escape is through the body and blood of Christ, with whom you are one body by communion through the Lord's Supper. You are one body with Christ by grace accessed through the measure of faith, which is a gift from God. Take the Lord's Supper daily, believing by faith that you are healed, and you'll see the manifestation of healing in your life through the grace of God. How do you know for sure that is true? The next chapter is going to show you how to get that knowledge and assurance.

CHAPTER 11
KNOW MEANS KNOW

And you shall know the truth, and the truth shall make you free.
John 8:32)

You don't know what you don't know. But you had better know the truth because Jesus said it will make you free. What does it mean to "know" the truth? The Greek word for "know" means to come to know. It also means to learn firsthand by personal experience. Knowledge is more than the learning of facts. True knowledge that will set you free is knowledge that is experienced firsthand.

That is what you're doing by reading this book. You're coming to know the truth about health and wellness once and for all. The rest of this book is going to focus on learning the truth through first-hand experience. Knowledge in and of itself is of little value unless it's applied. Hopefully, you've already started giving thanks before each meal and are honoring the body of Christ by taking the Lord's Supper often. You may already be seeing firsthand the changes that come from eating consecrated foods. The goal, however, is total and complete transformation:

Be transformed by the renewing of your mind. (Romans 12:2)

The Greek word for transformed means to change form. It's where we get our word "metamorphosis," which describes the trans-formation of a caterpillar into a butterfly. Transformation is not a minor change; It's a major and dramatic change of form, so much so that the new doesn't look much like the original, just like a butterfly looks nothing like a caterpillar when it is transformed. I want no less for you than that your health be transformed by the promises (truth) in the Bible, meaning that your health at the end of this process looks nothing like it did at the beginning.

If you have a sickness in your body, I want your body to be transformed by being completely healed. If you're in pain, I want your pain to go away. If you struggle with weight, I want your struggle to be over. I make no apologies that this book was written to help transform your health through the teachings of Jesus in a way that previous health books have been unable to do.

Some diet books encourage their readers to start by setting modest goals. Success for their diet is often nothing more than for the reader to reach a target weight. Many writers believe that eating the right foods and exercising regularly will solve all your health problems and their unique spin will be the difference. Most concede the best they can hope for is that some of their readers will make outward changes that might stick for an extended period of time.

My goals are much loftier than theirs. I want you to be completely healed in your body, soul, and spirit. If the Bible says that God wants to do something for you, then I'm not satisfied unless and until that promise is manifested in your life. You are going to take a big step towards that transformation in this chapter as you continue to learn the truth about diet and health.

Here are two truths: truth is true whether you know it or not, and truth is true even if you don't believe it. Truth only transforms when your mind is renewed. The problem is that humans use very little of their mind's capacity. Scientists say we only use five percent of our brain's capacity. That's a myth. You use all your brain capacity; you just don't perceive most of what your brain takes in. The brain processes eleven million bits of information every second, but you are only aware of approximately forty bits of information. Only forty out of eleven million bits of information. My wife would tell you there are many times when she is talking to me and I am not even processing that much!

You are capable of so much more. The human brain contains 2,500,000 gigabytes of storage space. The iPhone 7 only has 256 gigabytes. Why are we always on our phones? Our brains have so much more capacity to store information than our phones. If you were to place your brain's blood vessels end to end, they would stretch for more than 100,000 miles. It is only 24,906 miles around the entire world. The blood vessels in your brain would go around the world more than four times!

Information in your brain is traveling at 260 mph. The brain is confined to a small space, and, at 260 mph, it takes no time for information to travel from one side of it to the other. It is believed that there are a hundred billion neurons in the human brain, although one scientist said there were only eighty-six billion, and that sparked a huge debate. They finally agreed to disagree, so I'm sorry I can't give you the exact figure. I think they should count them and settle the issue once and for all. If they lose track, I must insist they start over because I want an accurate count of my neurons.

They do agree that bigger brains contain more neurons than smaller brains. I wonder how long it took them to figure that out. They should have asked me. I could have told them that bigger brains have more neurons and saved all the arguing. You don't need very many neurons to know that fact!

They all agree the brain makes a hundred trillion connections. I guess that is an easier number to calculate, so I won't make them count the connections, instead, I'll just take their word for it.

I read this about the capacity of the brain:

Propagating a nerve impulse, a distance of 1 millimeter requires about 5×10^{-15} joules. Because the total energy dissipated by the brain is about 10 watts, this means nerve impulses can collectively travel at most 2×10^{15} millimeters per second…It seems reasonable to conclude that the human brain has a raw computational power between 10^{13} and 10^{16} operations per second.

Get it. Got it. Good. I didn't get it. I would need to use more than forty of my eleven million bits to understand the above. Most of us are capable of understanding it if someone explained it properly. It might take years of study, but your brain is capable of understanding equations much harder than this one. That really is the point: we use very little of our brain capacity. We can know a lot more than we know.

Children have more neurons making connections than adults. If you have kids, you might find that hard to believe, but it's true. That's why it's easier for a child to learn a musical instrument or take up a sport like tennis. I read recently about an eleven-year-old who just graduated from college. He could probably easily explain the above concept of joules, synapses, and brain computational power. While he is certainly advanced beyond most, he still only uses a very small percentage of his brain's capacity.

Not all kids are as smart as the eleven-year-old college graduate. I read these test answers from children who didn't know the correct answer but somehow got a right answer anyway:

Question	Answer
What ended in 1896?	1895
How do you change centimeters to meters?	Remove the centi.
Where was Declaration of Independence Signed?	At the bottom.
The first cells were probably?	Lonely
Name six animals that live in the Arctic.	2 Polar Bears and 4 Seals
Bob has 36 candy bars. He eats 29. What does Bob have now?	Diabetes

One test question was, "Why does Saturn have three rings?" The child's answer was "Because God liked it, so he put a ring on it." I didn't get it until my wife explained to me that Beyoncé has a song with the line: "If you liked it, then you shoulda put a ring on it." According to that kid, God must have really liked Saturn because He put three rings on it!

A research study was done in Japan where they house the largest computer in the world. It has 705,204 processors and 1.4GB of RAM. It took that computer forty minutes to simulate one second of brain activity. I wonder how long it would take me to write this book, if I just used all my brain capacity for one minute! I'm sorry I am only using forty bits of information. I wish I used all eleven million bits because you would get a lot more out of this book. I do have help from the Holy Spirit, which makes a difference, but I wish I were doing more.

God gave us such tremendous brain capacity, and yet so many people don't believe in Him. How is that possible? It is because they don't really know Him. It doesn't matter how much knowledge you have; it takes more than brain capacity to really know God.

I was talking to a man who proudly proclaimed that he was an atheist. I said to him, "No, you're not. There's no such thing as an atheist." Offended, he argued back, "Yes, I am. Don't try to tell me what I believe." I told him that he can't be an atheist because it's impossible. He asked me why I would make such an outrageous statement, so I said to him, "You're an educated man. Out of all the information on the earth and in the universe, what percentage of information do you possess? Is it as much as ten percent or maybe even fifteen percent?" He said that it was nowhere near that high, and he speculated it was more like one-tenth of one percent.

I said to him, "So, you possess less than one-tenth of one percent of the entire information in the universe, and yet you state with certainty that, in the 99.9 percent of the information you admittedly don't possess, there's no possibility that God exists?" He conceded it was possible God could exist, but he still didn't believe He did. I told him he wasn't an atheist but an agnostic. An agnostic doesn't know if there is a God. That made sense to him and he conceded that I was right: it is impossible for anyone to be an atheist.

He was trying to know God based on his intellect and his five senses. You can't know God that way because it takes faith. God exists as a spirit, and you must know Him in the spiritual realm if you are to know Him at all. In John 4:24, Jesus said God is Spirit and His worshippers must worship Him in spirit and truth.

That's the problem: we only use a small part of our brain capacity, so our knowledge is very limited. We use even less of our faith, so our knowledge of God in the spiritual realm where truth resides is even more limited. That's why our food and diet plans don't work. They are confined to the natural world, of which we have limited and often faulty information. Faith can make up the difference, but most people's faith is very underdeveloped.

There's no way anyone can figure out the best diet or exercise plan for perfect health in the natural world and put it into a book. Divine health comes from the truth found in the spiritual realm accessed by faith. Here is what Isaiah said about food:

> Is anyone thirsty?
> Come and drink—
> even if you have no money!
> Come, take your choice of wine or milk—
> it's all free!
> Why spend your money on food that does not give you strength?
> Why pay for food that does you no good?
> Listen to me, and you will eat what is good.
> You will enjoy the finest food. (Isaiah 55:1–2 NLT)

"Why waste your money on food that does you no good and does not give you strength?" That is specifically my point: There is no food or drink you can buy that is good for your body. Some foods are better than others, but none are as good as the food God can provide. This is an invitation to feast at the table of God. There, you will enjoy the finest foods and will eat what is good for you. And it's free! Isaiah goes on to say:

> Come to me with your ears wide open.
> Listen, and you will find life.
> I will make an everlasting covenant with you.
> I will give you all the unfailing love I promised to David.
> (Isaiah 55:3 NLT)

He said to listen, and you will find life through an everlasting covenant. You have seen in previous chapters that the new and everlasting covenant came through Christ. In that covenant is the finest food that brings strength and wholeness. In the new covenant, health is not found in natural food and drink; it is found in the unfailing love of God. Isaiah then reveals what we should listen to:

> "My thoughts are nothing like your thoughts," says the Lord.
> "And my ways are far beyond anything you could imagine.
> For just as the heavens are higher than the earth,
> so my ways are higher than your ways
> and my thoughts higher than your thoughts." (Isaiah 55:8–9 NLT)

This tells you that what you need to know are the ways of God. The difficulty in knowing God's ways is that His thoughts are nothing like your thoughts and His ways are beyond anything you can imagine. Because His ways are higher and His thoughts are higher than your thoughts, you must think beyond your own thoughts and the teachings of man. You find God's thoughts in His word. God's word is what you feast on to produce divine health:

> It is the same with my word.
> I send it out, and it always produces fruit.
> It will accomplish all I want it to,
> and it will prosper everywhere I send it. (Isaiah 55:11 NLT)

God's word will accomplish all He wants it to accomplish and will bring prosperity everywhere He sends His word. Isaiah didn't have the complete Bible like we have today. Jesus had not yet appeared on this earth, but Jesus was still giving Isaiah a revelation about life. Notice in verse eight it says that the Lord is the one speaking. Jesus was speaking this revelation about spiritual food to Isaiah, bringing divine health long before He ever appeared on the earth.

God's word is the food that brings life to our soul. Jesus is called the Word in John 1. When Jesus said that the truth shall make you free, He told us how to know the truth. He said you will know the truth if you abide in My word. It is in God's word that our mind is transformed, and we know the truth.

I have said in previous chapters that Jesus is the one who is going to provide you with the food that will produce divine health. It was that way even for the children of Israel. Look at what Paul said in his letter to the church of Corinth:

> Moreover, brethren, I do not want you to be unaware that all our fathers were under the cloud, all passed through the sea, all were baptized into Moses in the cloud and in the sea, all ate the same spiritual food, and all drank the same spiritual drink. For they drank of that spiritual Rock that followed them, and that Rock was Christ. (1 Corinthians 10: 1–4)

Paul said that when the children of Israel were in the wilderness, they were eating spiritual food and drinking spiritual drink that came from the Rock, and the Rock was Christ. The food and drink they ate in the natural realm, was actually the supernatural food given to them by Christ. Even in the Old Testament, Jesus was supplying their food and supernaturally transforming it to give them divine health!

In the new covenant, the food you eat in the natural realm is not what you were meant to eat. You're to eat the spiritual food only Jesus can provide. While you eat natural food, it becomes supernatural when it comes from Jesus:

> The eyes of all look to you in hope;
> you give them their food as they need it.
> When you open your hand,
> you satisfy the hunger and thirst of every living thing.
> (Psalm 145:15-16 NLT)

> You satisfy me more than the richest feast.
> I will praise you with songs of joy.
> (Psalm 63:5 NLT)

Only God can satisfy the hunger and thirst of every living thing. Is the spiritual food more satisfying to you than the richest foods you can eat? That is what you need to know: God wants to be your supply. He wants to satisfy your hunger and thirst and give you food as you need it.

Do you remember how God commanded that the children of Israel were not to eat an animal that died of itself? For obvious reasons, the dead animal could have a disease that might harm them. God told them to sell those animals in the marketplace; in other words, to sell them to unbelievers. God was not concerned about the health of pagans, and they could eat anything they wanted and suffer whatever sicknesses came upon them. God's concern was for His people. He did not want them to eat anything that would harm them.

The same is true for us today. Reread 1 Timothy 4:3–5):

Forbidding to marry, and commanding to abstain from foods which God created to be received with thanksgiving by those who believe and know the truth. For every creature of God is good, and nothing is to be refused if it is received with thanksgiving; for it is sanctified by the word of God and prayer.

Do you believe what Paul said in this verse, that if you say a prayer of thanksgiving before every meal, then the food becomes consecrated and is good for you to eat? Verse three says this is only for those who believe and who know the truth. You know the truth now because I have outlined it for you in the previous chapters. The question is: Do you believe it?

Today, when an unbeliever goes to the grocery store and buys something off the shelf, it is what it is. That food may or may not be healthy for him. If you buy that same food and receive it with thanksgiving, that food is consecrated and healthy for your body. That same food produces different results based on who purchased it. If you buy that food and don't consecrate it, you will get the same results as an unbeliever. If you are in a restaurant and the waitress serves your meal, that meal is consecrated if you give thanks before you eat it, and it is beneficial to your body. That meal could have just as easily gone to the table of an unbeliever and caused sickness. You avoided the sickness because of your relationship with God.

Do you believe that God wants something different for you than He wants for the world? That's why He wants us to reject the world's views on health and wellness. He is perfectly capable of protecting you and showing you the truth without relying on unbelievers.

I am asserting in this book, backed by Scripture, that food is consecrated by receiving it with thanksgiving and God uses consecrated food to heal your body. I have also asserted that the Lord's Supper is to be observed often and the honoring of the body of Christ brings health and wellness to your body. If those things are true, and I'm convinced they are, then they have the potential to bring total transformation to your body. However, the scripture is clear that you will not be transformed unless your mind is renewed. Your mind cannot be renewed unless you are open to the truth.

Why do we give thanks for the food? Because Jesus is the source of the food and drink. Do you truly believe Jesus came to provide salvation for you and abundant life on this earth and He is to be the source for your food and drink? If so, do you believe Jesus can transform your health through the food?

The Pharisees had a hard time believing Jesus was who He said He was. They were constantly questioning Him and trying to get Him to say something they could use to kill Him. One day, Jesus said something that really set them off. Read Luke 5:18–25:

> Then behold, men brought on a bed a man who was paralyzed, whom they sought to bring in and lay before Him. And when they could not find how they might bring him in, because of the crowd, they went up on the housetop and let him down with his bed through the tiling into the midst before Jesus.
>
> When He saw their faith, He said to him, "Man, your sins are forgiven you."
>
> And the scribes and the Pharisees began to reason, saying, "Who is this who speaks blasphemies? Who can forgive sins but God alone?"
>
> But when Jesus perceived their thoughts, He answered and said to them, "Why are you reasoning in your hearts? Which is easier, to say, 'Your sins are forgiven you,' or to say, 'Rise up and walk'?
>
> But that you may know that the Son of Man has power on earth to forgive sins"—He said to the man who was paralyzed, "I say to you, arise, take up your bed, and go to your house."
>
> Immediately he rose up before them, took up what he had been lying on, and departed to his own house, glorifying God.

The man was paralyzed. We don't know why he couldn't walk, but his condition was such that he had to be carried in on a bed. Jesus saw their faith and told the man He forgave him of his sins. The Pharisees went ballistic, saying, "Who are you to forgive sins?" Jesus answered, "Which is easier, to forgive sins or to heal the man?"

I can answer that question. It is much easier to say He forgave him of his sins because it can't be proven one way or the other. It is much harder to heal the man because you would know immediately if Jesus had the power to heal him. You would see the manifestation of healing in the natural right away. Jesus healed the man so they would know He also had the power to forgive the man of his sins.

We struggle with the same unbelief, especially when it comes to our health. We have a hard time believing God can heal our bodies. To be more specific, we generally believe God can heal our bodies; we just aren't sure He will. I believe that, not only will God heal our bodies but that He wants to. Is it easier to believe that God will heal your body or that God will save you from your sins?

Look at what you had to believe to be saved. The jailer asked Paul what he needed to do to be saved (Acts 16:30). Paul said to believe in Jesus, and you will be saved. All you have to do is believe, and all your sins are forgiven, and you will spend an eternity in heaven. A simple prayer can secure your eternal destiny.

Why is it so hard to believe that a simple prayer of thanksgiving can transform your food? Why is it so hard to believe that the Lord's Supper can restore your health?

Look at the man who was paralyzed. All Jesus said was, "Take up your pallet and walk." Immediately, the man walked. His spine that was severed was miraculously restored to complete health. As much as doctors have studied spinal cord injuries, they have never developed an operation that could fix a severed spine. Jesus did it by speaking six words!

How hard is it to believe that the blind man was healed? In one second, Jesus spoke words of healing, and whatever disease he had, his eyes were completely restored. What about the withered hand? With a few words, the tendons, cartilage, and bone structure were all made as good as new. If you were to tear an ACL in your knee, it would take surgery and nine months of rehab to get you back to normal. Jesus spoke a few words, and the entire biological makeup of a person was completely transformed.

Do you believe that happened? If you believe Jesus did those things for them, why is it hard to believe He will do it for you? Which is easier to believe: that your sins are forgiven or that Jesus can heal you? Here is another truth: neither will happen if you don't believe. It will not work, if you don't believe it will work. Look at what it says in Hebrews 4:2:

> For indeed the gospel was preached to us as well as to them; but the word which they heard did not profit them, not being mixed with faith in those who heard it.

You can't know the truth until you believe it, and you can't receive it until you believe it. The Jesus Diet will be of no benefit to you if you don't believe it. Everything God does for us is grace given to us through Jesus Christ. That is the gospel, and that is the good news. However, it will not profit you if it is not mixed with faith when you hear it or, in this case, when you read it.

The Greek word *know* also implies intimacy. It was often used in the Bible to describe the sexual relationship between a man and a woman. When a couple had marital relations, they knew each other. To know the truth means to understand it and to have an intimate relationship with the truth.

It has another meaning in science. It is literally to learn facts and to believe them. Once you learn a fact and you accept it as true, then you know it. As it relates to God, the truths are unseen, which is why it takes faith:

> Now it came to pass, as He sat at the table with them, that He took bread, blessed and broke it, and gave it to them. Then their eyes were opened, and they knew Him; and He vanished from their sight. (Luke 24:30–31)

After Jesus's ascension, the disciples spent time with Jesus not knowing it was Him. When He took the bread, blessed it, and broke it, they immediately recognized Him. It says they knew Jesus through the breaking of bread. That is my prayer for you: that you will know Jesus through the breaking of your bread and will really know Him in the most intimate way possible. In that knowing, you will be transformed.

CHAPTER 12
GIVE THANKS, DISCERN, REPEAT

I still have many things to say to you, but you cannot bear them
now. However, when He, the Spirit of truth, has come, He will guide
you into all truth.
(John 16:12-13)

Many products come with washing and drying instructions, warning labels, and general instructions on how to care for the item.
Some of these instructions are rather strange, to say the least.

A container of dog pills has this instruction: "May cause drowsiness. Use care when operating a car or heavy machinery." A warning
label on a children's cough medicine says the same thing: "Do not
drive or operate heavy machinery after taking this medicine." All
dogs and children should always use caution when driving a car or
operating heavy machinery whether they take the medications or
not!

A Nytol sleep aid warning label says: "May cause drowsiness."
Isn't that why you bought the product? A knife sharpener comes
with the obvious warning: "Knives are sharp." A similar warning is
on a coffee cup: "Hot coffee is hot." A package of bread pudding
says: "Pudding will be hot after heating." Thanks for the warnings,
but I don't need them. I'm not a scientist, but most things are hot
after heating, most things sharp are sharp, and most things hot are
hot.

A hair dryer can be hot, but not always; it's not hot when it's not on. How do you create a warning label for that reality? You could warn: "Hair Dryer is hot when it's hot." One comes with the following warning label: "Do not use while sleeping." How do you read the warning label if you're asleep? I don't know how many times I've used a hairdryer when I was asleep, but I'll try to remember to read the warning label if I do. Here is an obvious warning on a blowtorch: "Do not use for drying your hair." You also don't want to dry your hair with a blowtorch while you are sleeping!

A shirt has this tag: "Do not iron while you're wearing this shirt." I don't iron, so I don't need the warning label for me. However, my wonderful wife takes care of the ironing, and she needs to know this. I don't want her to iron my shirt while I'm wearing it!

A toaster comes with the warning: "Do not use underwater." I thought at first it was because the toast would get soggy, but it's actually because of electrical shock. That makes a lot of sense. I don't want wet toast, but I also don't want to get electrocuted when I put the toaster underwater. Here's more good advice on a box of fireworks: "Do not put in mouth." I can see why you don't want to put fireworks in your mouth. You don't want to use fireworks underwater either!

On Apple's website is a warning: "Do not eat iPod shuffle." Okay, I won't. On a hanger is the warning label: "Do not swallow." That's another good warning. I can see where you wouldn't want to swallow a hanger. You also wouldn't want to stick a hanger in your ear, and I wonder why they don't have a warning label for that possibility. A mattress has the label: "Do not attempt to swallow." I didn't realize swallowing hangers and mattresses were becoming a problem. Apparently, they are not teaching these things in our schools.

A bag of Fritos advertised: "Prize inside! You could be a winner. No purchase necessary. Details inside." Did they just give me permission to open the bag without having to buy it? If there is no prize, can I close it back up and open the next bag until I find the one with a prize? A Christmas lights package instructs that they are for "indoor or outdoor use only." I am glad they cleared that up because it's nice to not have too many options.

A pilot's seat in the airplane says: "Seat must be facing forward at take-off." Seriously! If the pilot needs that warning label, I don't want him flying any plane I am on. A chainsaw has a picture with a warning label: "Do not hold on the wrong end." That seems obvious to me, but I guess not. It should also have the warning label: "Do not cut off your arm or leg!"

A skin cream has the warning label: "Avoid contact with your eyes, ears, brain." How could it come in contact with my brain? Never mind, I don't want to know. A bottle of hair dye says: "Do not use as an ice cream topping!" I'm glad for the warning because I was considering it. A can of spray paint warns: "Do not spray on face." A can of mace warns: "May irritate eyes." They must put these warning labels on these products for a reason. Maybe I have overestimated the collective IQ of our country.

Some labels are not for warnings but are for educational purposes. An egg carton says: "Contains eggs," and a package of peanuts says: "Contains nuts." A kettle instructs the user how to turn it on: "The kettle is turned on by turning the on/off switch to on." All good information. A five-hundred-piece jigsaw puzzle says: "Some assembly required." I'm never buying a puzzle again because I refuse to buy anything that requires assembly. I don't buy furniture, kid's toys, and now, I guess, puzzles, since they require assembly.

Here's a very useful warning label: "If you cannot read what's on this label, then do not use this product." They should have that on every warning label. If you don't know how to read, don't use the product.

It's clear we need instructions. When Jesus was raised from the dead, until the time He ascended into heaven, He spent much of His time giving the disciples instructions on what to do after He was gone. One of the instructions was:

Do not leave Jerusalem, but wait for the gift my Father promised, which you have heard me speak about. For John baptized with water, but in a few days, you will be baptized with the Holy Spirit. (Acts 1:4–5 NIV)

He had already spoken to them about the Holy Spirit, and now He was telling them to stay in Jerusalem because they were going to be baptized with the Holy Spirit. Here is one of the things Jesus had previously said to them about the Holy Spirit:

Nevertheless, I tell you the truth. It is to your advantage that I go away; for if I do not go away, the Helper will not come to you; but if I depart, I will send Him to you. (John 16:7)

What could be better than being with Jesus? For three years, the disciples had spent almost every waking minute with Him. They had seen Him perform all kinds of miracles and spent countless hours listening to His teachings. It must have been very confusing for them to hear Him say they would be better off if He left them. Why would they be better off?

But you will receive **power** when the Holy Spirit comes on you; and you will be my witnesses in Jerusalem, and in all Judea and Samaria, and to the ends of the earth. (Acts 1:8 NIV) (Emphasis Added)

The Greek word for *power* here is "dynamis." It's where we get the word dynamite. It's a miraculous power, and a power that comes through God's ability. The disciples already had power through Jesus's name. They could heal the sick, raise the dead, and cast out demons, but that power had some limitations. Up until this time, the Holy Spirit would only come upon people to give them the power to perform certain functions. Something dramatic was about to happen to them and was going to change the entire world. Not only would the Holy Spirit come upon them, but He would come to live inside of them:

But if the Spirit of Him who raised Jesus from the dead dwells in you, He who raised Christ from the dead will also give life to your mortal bodies through His Spirit who dwells in you. (Romans 8:11)

The Spirit of God, God Himself, one part of the three-person Trinity, would live inside of the disciples. When He did, they were going to be endued with power. It is the same Spirit with the same power that raised Jesus from the dead. That same Spirit was roaming around the earth at creation (Genesis 1:2). Job 33:4 said it was the Spirit of God who made us. The power that created the world, created our bodies, and raised Jesus from the dead was going to be made available to the disciples. Not only would the Spirit of God live inside of the disciples, but that gift was available to everyone who believed:

Then Peter said to them, "Repent, and let every one of you be baptized in the name of Jesus Christ for the remission of sins; and you shall receive the gift of the Holy Spirit. For the promise is to you and to your children, and to all who are afar off, as many as the Lord our God will call." (Acts 2:38–39)

It is the new covenant. God sent His Holy Spirit to dwell in every believer from Jesus's death forward, and that includes you and me. We have living inside of us the same power that lived inside of the disciples. Not only that, but we have Jesus speaking to us through the Holy Spirit:

"I have much more to say to you, more than you can now bear. But when he, the Spirit of truth, comes, he will guide you into all the truth. He will not speak on his own; he will speak only what he hears, and he will tell you what is yet to come. He will glorify me because it is from me that he will receive what he will make known to you. All that belongs to the Father is mine. That is why I said the Spirit will receive from me what he will make known to you." (John 16:12–15 NIV)

Jesus said He has many things to tell us and that it's better for Him to go away because the Holy Spirit will come and live inside of us and speak to us and guide us into all truth. What will He speak? He will only speak what He hears. What does He hear? He hears Jesus speaking what Jesus wants to make known to us. Jesus will speak to the Holy Spirit, and the Holy Spirit will tell us what He said and will guide us into all truth. Once Jesus ascended, this process began:

> I wrote about all that Jesus began to do and to teach until the day he was taken up to heaven, after giving instructions through the Holy Spirit to the apostles he had chosen. (Acts 1:1–2 NIV)

While He was alive, Jesus gave them instructions in person. After He had ascended, Jesus continued to give them instructions through the Holy Spirit.

JESUS DIET PRINCIPLE #7

Listen to the Holy Spirit. It is Jesus speaking to you, giving you instructions on how to have an abundant life.

Jesus continues to give us instructions today through the Holy Spirit because He has the responsibility to keep us in the will of God until the last day, when He will raise us up. Reread what Jesus said in John 6:38–40 (NIV):

> For I have come down from heaven not to do my will but to do the will of him who sent me. And this is the will of him who sent me, that I shall lose none of all those he has given me but raise them up at the last day. For my Father's will is that everyone who looks to the Son and believes in him shall have eternal life, and I will raise them up at the last day.

Jesus said He was sent on this earth to do the will of God the Father. What was the will of the Father? That Jesus would die on the cross for our sins, sicknesses, and sorrows and be raised from the dead to conquer sin and death. This provides the basis for a new covenant between God and man based on the body and blood of Jesus: so that everyone who believed in Jesus would gain eternal life. When Jesus died on the cross, the work of providing salvation was finished. However, Jesus's work was not done. The Father has also given Him the task of keeping those who believe safe until the last day. He cannot lose any who believe. He is talking about you and me. Jesus has the responsibility to make sure we make it to the last day safe and sound.

So, Jesus sent the Holy Spirit to live inside of us. Jesus knew we needed the same power He had living inside of Him. Remember, at Jesus's baptism, the Holy Spirit descended upon Jesus like a dove, and the Holy Spirit came and lived inside of Jesus. That's how He was able to do miracles. He raised the dead, healed the sick, opened blind eyes, caused the lame to walk, and taught with such power and conviction because of the power of the Holy Spirit living inside of Him. You have and need that same power.

At the same time, you need help living this life. You are faced with too many challenges and troubles. With the Holy Spirit living inside of you, you have a conduit for Jesus to speak through. Anything Jesus wants to tell you, He can tell you immediately through the Holy Spirit.

Jesus speaks to you all the time, giving you instructions. I cringe every time I hear someone say something like, "Why has God left me? Why won't God answer my prayers? I feel so alone. God, I don't know what to do. God doesn't care about me. God is punishing me. I can't hear anything from God. God doesn't hear my prayers."

We say things like that because we don't understand who lives inside of us. You have everything you need for abundant life right inside of you through the person of the Holy Spirit. You have His power available to you anytime you need it. That's why Jesus said that if you have the faith of a mustard seed, you can move a mountain. You have that power to move a mountain living inside of you. You don't have to wait on God to heal your body because Jesus has already made that provision for you, and the power to heal your body is living inside of you right now. You don't have to wait on God to deliver you from the works of Satan, because Jesus has already made that provision and the power to cast out demons lives inside of you. You even have the power inside of you to raise someone from the dead if need be:

> As His divine power has given to us all things that pertain to life and godliness, through the knowledge of Him who called us by glory and virtue. (2 Peter 1:3)

That divine power has given us ALL things that pertain to life and godliness. All means all. How do you get that power? Through the knowledge of Him who called you. Where do you get the knowledge? Jesus speaks to the Holy Spirit, who then tells you what He said, and then you know what to do.

Why don't you do it? Because you have to get what is in your spirit into your flesh so you can act on it. 1 Thessalonians 5:23 (NIV) says:

> May God himself, the God of peace, sanctify you through and through. May your whole spirit, soul and body be kept blameless at the coming of our Lord Jesus Christ.

God wants to sanctify you through and through. This verse says that you are a three-part being: spirit, soul, and body. God wants you to be kept blameless until the coming of our Lord Jesus Christ. It is Jesus's responsibility to teach you everything you need to know in order to be sanctified in all three parts of your body.

Your spirit is already perfect (Hebrews 12:23; Hebrews 10:10; 2 Corinthians 5:21). First John 3:9 says everyone that is born of God, cannot sin. Your spirit cannot sin because it is one hundred percent perfect. It is holy, righteous, perfect, ready for heaven. You can go into the throne of God with confidence because your spirit has been transformed.

Your body needs to be transformed in the same way your spirit is transformed. The whole key to abundant life is getting what is in your spirit into your flesh so that your flesh stops doing things that are harmful to you. How does that happen? Jesus tells the Holy Spirit what you need to do, and then the Holy Spirit tells you. How does the Holy Spirit tell you? Through your soul, which is your mind and emotions. Romans 12:2 says that you are transformed by the renewing of your mind:

> And do not be conformed to this world, but be transformed by the renewing of your mind, that you may prove what is that good and acceptable and perfect will of God.

When your mind is renewed, it is transformed. What is transformed? Your flesh is transformed. It is transformed into knowing what the perfect will of God is for your life. Then the process of sanctification in your spirit, soul, and body is complete.

Here is the process:

1. Jesus knows what you need to do about anything pertaining to life and godliness.

2. He gives you instructions through the Holy Spirit. He tells the Holy Spirit what He wants you to know, and the Holy Spirit tells you.

3. If you believe it by faith, then your mind is renewed. When your mind is renewed, then your soul is made perfect like your spirit is perfect in that area. It then transforms your flesh. Slowly but surely, you are transformed in your flesh into the likeness of Christ.

As it pertains to the Jesus Diet, Jesus is going to give you personalized instructions on what to do to transform your health. I have purposefully avoided personal examples and practical suggestions in this book. Jesus has given me many instructions on how to be healthy. I don't want to tell you what those instructions are because

I don't want you to think the way to health is to do what I'm doing. Those are my instructions. Yours may be different. I want to give you what the word of God says, and then you should let Jesus instruct you on what you should eat and what you should drink. I want Jesus to tell you what books you should read and what exercises you should do. I want Jesus to tell you whose advice you should heed.

The world is full of books with practical suggestions. There's nothing wrong with them, but I want you to get your instructions directly from the Holy Spirit because He's getting them directly from Jesus. That's why you must reject the world's system of health, diets, and exercise. Why would you think you can get any advice from the world on life and godliness? Why would you think some diet that Lady Gaga follows would be good for you just because she does it? What does the government know about divine health? What can the surgeon general tell you that the Great Physician can't tell you through the Holy Spirit?

Read 1 John 2:27 in the NASB:

As for you, the anointing which you received from Him abides in you, and you have no need for anyone to teach you; but as His anointing teaches you about all things, and is true and is not a lie, and just as it has taught you, you abide in Him.

You don't have any need for any man to teach you. The anointing (Holy Spirit), which abides in you, will teach you everything you need to know. What He teaches you is true and is not a lie, and you can count on it. So, abide in Christ, and He abides in you, and your life will be transformed if you follow the instructions that He teaches you.

You don't need me to teach you anything in this book. That's not to say that this book can't be helpful, or you don't need to read other Christian or non-Christian writers. However, the Holy Spirit has to be the one who teaches you something through this book.

There has to be something in this book that Jesus wants you to know for Him to use it to help you to renew your mind. The primary things He wants you to know are right there in His word.

You have already seen how giving thanks before every meal and properly discerning the Lord's body through the Lord's Supper will transform your health. I believe Jesus is using this book to help many people renew their minds to those two truths, and their lives will be transformed as a result. But you need more than those two truths. You need ongoing instructions on how to live your life to produce and to maintain divine health.

I can also say with confidence and certainty that Jesus wants you to be healthy. If you don't know that, I hope your mind is renewed by reading this book. Jesus died for your health. He took your sicknesses upon Himself, and now He is taking the responsibility for sustaining your health. If you need to lose weight and your weight is causing health problems, Jesus is going to give the Holy Spirit specific instructions as to what you need to do to lose the weight. If you are sick, Jesus will give you specific instructions on what you are to do to be healed. He will lead you to the right doctor if that is what you need. He will lead you to the right book if that is what you need. Jesus can use anything to lead you to divine health.

And He also uses other members of the body of Christ to help us. All you have to do is listen to the Holy Spirit and follow the instructions by faith when He is speaking to others on your behalf. Notice what happened to Paul when he did not listen to the instructions of the Spirit told to Paul's friends:

And finding disciples, we stayed there seven days. They told Paul through the Spirit not to go up to Jerusalem. (Acts 21:4)

And as we stayed many days, a certain prophet named Agabus came down from Judea. When he had come to us, he took Paul's belt, bound his own hands and feet, and said, "Thus says the Holy Spirit, 'So shall the Jews at Jerusalem bind the man who owns this belt, and deliver him into the hands of the Gentiles.'" (Acts 21:10–11)

The disciples and Agabus all warned Paul through the Spirit not to go to Jerusalem. Agabus had a vision that Paul would be bound and delivered into the hands of the Gentiles. Here was Paul's response:

> Now when we heard these things, both we and those from that place pleaded with him not to go up to Jerusalem. Then Paul answered, "What do you mean by weeping and breaking my heart? For I am ready not only to be bound, but also to die at Jerusalem for the name of the Lord Jesus." (Acts 21: 12–13)

You have to admire Paul's courage; however, he was not following the instructions of the Holy Spirit and that was foolish. I'm sorry to say that about Paul because he was one of the greatest men who ever lived. I have tremendous respect for Paul and can't wait to meet him in heaven, but unlike Jesus, he wasn't perfect. He didn't always follow the instructions of the Holy Spirit perfectly, and it got him into unnecessary trouble. Remember, the Holy Spirit only speaks what Jesus tells Him to speak. Jesus warned Paul through the Holy Spirit not to go to Jerusalem because He knew what would happen if he did. He even told Paul through the prophet that if he went, he would end up in prison. Paul went anyway and was thrown into prison for more than two years.

Jesus is going to give you specific instructions related to your health, and I encourage you to follow them. At the same time, always remember that you are under grace just like Paul was under grace. Even though he went to Jerusalem when the Spirit was telling him not to go, God still used him to preach the gospel, and He protected him. Even though Paul was beaten and nearly torn in two by the mob, he didn't lose his life. He suffered more than he had to because he didn't follow the instructions, but Jesus was still giving him new instructions while he was in Jerusalem. Jesus never gives up on you, and He is going to keep working with you so he can get you to the day of His coming. Even when you get off track, He will give you instructions to get back on track.

Most of us ignore those instructions. We walk by the flesh and not by the spirit. Consequently, we are sick, weak, and dying prematurely. Jesus will transform your health, your body, your mind, your emotions, your diet, your sicknesses, your pains, and your sorrows if you follow His instructions. And His instructions are not a secret. You just need to listen and believe them by faith. The Holy Spirit will provide the power to make them come to pass and the wisdom to know what to do:

> If any of you lacks wisdom, you should ask God, who gives generously to all without finding fault, and it will be given to you. But when you ask, you must believe and not doubt, because the one who doubts is like a wave of the sea, blown and tossed by the wind. (James 1:5–6 NIV)

God gives wisdom generously without fault if you need it. But you must ask for it and believe it without a doubt. If you lack wisdom and ask for it, God will tell Jesus what you need to do, Jesus will tell the Holy Spirit, and then the Holy Spirit will tell you. This process has worked for generations and will continue until Jesus comes again. God will give you all the wisdom you need generously. What if the reason you need wisdom is that you did something stupid? James said God will give you wisdom without finding fault. Your health may be a mess because of your own choices. In fact, it probably is. But God still wants to bring healing and divine health to you regardless of whose fault it is. He will generously give you the wisdom you need to restore your health by speaking through the Holy Spirit.

How do you know if it is really the Holy Spirit speaking? Does it line up with what God's Word says? The Holy Spirit will never contradict the Bible. It also must line up with the new covenant. The

Holy Spirit is never going to put you back under a set of laws. For instance, the Holy Spirit is never going to say to you that you can never eat a specific food, because that would contradict what Jesus said when He made all foods clean. However, the Holy Spirit will work with you based on your faith.

For instance, if you have a gluten sensitivity, or worse, you have Crohn's disease, the Holy Spirit may advise you not to eat gluten. The power to be healed from Crohn's disease is inside of you, and Jesus has already made the provision, but you may not be strong enough in your faith and in the renewing of your mind to receive total healing. Consequently, you will get sick eating gluten until you can receive your healing. The Holy Spirit may very well give you instructions that will help you, and you should follow those until you are completely healed. Paul basically said the same thing to Timothy:

> No longer drink only water but use a little wine for your stomach's sake and your frequent infirmities. (1 Timothy 5:23)

Timothy was obviously getting sick from drinking the water. Paul gave him some practical advice: don't drink the water; drink wine instead. In the same way, Jesus is going to give you specific instructions through the Holy Spirit that will help you on a day-to-day basis.

Here is what you should do: Give thanks before every meal and receive with thanksgiving every piece of food you put in your mouth and every single drink that you drink. Discern the Lord's body with every meal and see every piece of food as the body of Christ, which was broken for your healing. Every time you eat, remember that Jesus's broken body secured your healing. Every time you drink of the cup, remember that Jesus's blood was shed for you for the remission of your sins. Thank Jesus at every meal for His broken body and His shed blood.

Give thanks, honor, and repeat. Repeat over and over again. Then follow whatever other instructions Jesus gives you through the Holy Spirit. Then you will be transformed, and you will start to see miracles happen in your life. You will see sicknesses go away and your body transformed. You will see your body for what it is: The Temple of the Holy Spirit. It is where the Holy Spirit dwells. Then your body will honor God:

Or do you not know that your body is the temple of the Holy Spirit who is in you, whom you have from God, and you are not your own? For you were bought at a price; therefore, glorify God in your body¹and in your spirit, which are God's.
(1 Corinthians 6:19–20).

PART THREE

THE JESUS DIET WEIGHT LOSS AND WELLNESS PLAN

CHAPTER 13
REMOVE THE SCALES FROM YOUR EYES AND YOUR HOUSE

Then the eyes of both of them were opened... (Genesis 3:7)

(I hope you aren't superstitious about the number thirteen because this is one of the most important practical chapters in this book).

I realized early on that you can't write a book about health without a chapter on weight loss. The problem is that the Bible is completely silent about the subject. There are passages in the old testament about gluttony, but gluttony and the need for weight loss were not mentioned by Jesus. Ironically, the only mention of gluttony was when Jesus was accused of being a glutton by the Pharisees.

How do you write about weight loss from the teachings of Jesus when He never mentions it? Or did He? More on that later.

As I mentioned earlier, Americans spend more than sixty billion dollars a year on weight-loss products and services. They spend more than that annually on weight-related illnesses. Efforts to change those statistics are not working. Americans spend more per capita on health care than any other country and are one of the unhealthiest developed countries. There are fitness centers everywhere, yet sixty-seven percent of gym memberships go unused. More than forty-five percent of Americans are on a diet at any one time, as

I documented earlier, and yet ninety-five percent of all diets fail, so the wasted effort is not making a dent in the problem.

Because diet and exercise plans fail, Americans have turned to cosmetic surgery as another way to change their appearance. Americans spent sixteen billion dollars a year, and there were 17.7 million cosmetic procedures in 2017. In 1997, there were only 101,176 breast augmentation surgeries compared to 2016, when there were 310,444, an increase of more than three hundred percent. There were 4,597,886 Botox procedures in 2016, but only 66,167 in 1997, which is a huge increase.

Do you know what Botox really is? It is a strain of botulism mostly known as a deadly food poisoning. The poison is shot into your skin, where it paralyzes facial muscles. I wonder who was the first person to test it out? They say there are no long-term effects, but how do they really know?

And the procedures are getting stranger and stranger every year. There is a new procedure called Hi Def Liposculpture. It is where doctors surgically sculpt the abdominal area to create a six-pack, washboard look. The problem, among other things, is that if the person gains weight, which they almost always do, the body fat covers up the six-pack just like it did before the surgery.

There is the grin lift. Apparently, our smiles droop as we age. This surgery cuts certain muscles around the mouth to prevent drooping. It's also used for those who have a permanent scowl. Unfortunately, if the surgery is not successful, the recipient ends up looking like the Joker from Batman, which I think is worse than a droopy smile.

There is the belly button procedure. It is for those who want to change their belly button from an outie to an innie or vice versa. There is the chipmunk cheek procedure for those whose cheeks are too chubby. One of the comments I get most about my new granddaughter is how cute her chubby cheeks are. Apparently, they aren't so cute when you get older.

There is the gummy procedure. This is for those whose smile reveals too much of their gums. The surgeons cut the muscles that elevate the lip and insert a space implant above the lip to prevent the muscles from reconnecting.

There is the eyebrow transplant, which surgically replaces hair in the eyebrows. My wife says my eyebrows make me look angry all the time, even though I am rarely angry. Maybe plastic surgery could fix that problem. I remember my sisters plucking their eyebrows because they had too much hair. Now you can have them removed by waxing or by laser surgery.

You can change the color of your eyes with eye implants, with many colors to choose from, including a zebra print. I think I will pass and stick with my baby-blue eyes. Some professional poker players get plastic surgery to create a stone face, so they don't give away their poker hands with their facial expressions.

In Japan, you can have surgery on your palms to change the lines. Supposedly, this will change your fate. If your previous lines showed you were going to die prematurely, then the plastic surgeon can extend the lines and hopefully extend your life expectancy. Somebody needs to tell them it's a waste of money. The Bible says our days are numbered by God.

Do you like your voice? If you don't, you can change it for the cost of a hospital visit and doctor's fee. Be advised that the surgeon cuts open your neck and alters your vocal cords with implants and injections. This is primarily for those with squeaky voices who want a deeper voice. I wonder if they can make my singing voice sound like Pavarotti's. If so, it might be something to consider.

My sisters used to go crazy over guys with dimples. Thanks to scientific breakthroughs, you can have artificial dimples put in your face. They aren't real, they only give the illusion of dimples, but it might have the same effect on women, although I'm not sure. I don't have dimples and my beautiful wife is crazy about me, so I don't think it is necessary for me anyway.

There is a procedure called Bilame prelamination. It's where a nose is constructed somewhere on a body other than where the nose normally goes. The surgeon takes tissue from other parts of the body and sculpts them into what looks like a nose. I saw a picture of a man who had a nose constructed on his forehead. It was upside down! God did not make our noses facing up because of the problems we would have when it rains. I am not sure if those noses have the same problem, but they certainly look strange.

You can also have ears constructed on other parts of your body. I saw another picture of a man with ears on his forearms. I am thankful I have never run into anyone who has had a nose or ear put on a different part of his body. I hope I never do.

I have unfortunately seen people who have had this plastic surgery: tongue bifurcation. This is where your tongue is cut down the middle and split in two. I read an article where someone explained that he did it because he wanted to look like a lizard. Others do it because they want to look like a snake. I've never had the desire to look like either reptile, and I hope neither have your kids.

Some people become obsessed with surgeries and are addicted to changing their appearance. I saw a picture of one lady who has had more than a hundred surgeries to make herself look like a Barbie doll. Another man has had several surgeries to look like Brittany Spears. I saw a picture, and he looked nothing like her. I'm not sure why he would want to look like her anyway. Brittany Spears will not look like Brittany Spears in a few years when the aging process kicks in. I'm sure she will have plastic surgeries to slow the process down, but it will happen, nonetheless.

One lady has had four nose jobs, four boob jobs, a butt lift, a cheek alteration, two liposuctions, and several other surgeries. Her breasts were augmented to a size 30J, and she had six ribs removed so her waist could be reduced to a size twenty-four. She wanted to look like a cartoon character. She even had the color of her eyes changed to a cartoon green. I saw a picture of her as well, and I wish I hadn't.

Before you run out and get one of those surgeries, you should know that twenty percent of all people who have plastic surgery regret it immediately. Did you know women are more likely to attempt suicide if they have had plastic surgery? Women with breast implants were two times more likely to commit suicide than those who have never had their breasts augmented. Psychologists believe it's because they have lost their self-identification. I think it's because they are deceived. They were deceived from the moment they thought they needed it. It is informative to know that the rate of attempted suicides does not rise for those women who have breast augmentation because of health reasons such as mastectomies. Their percentage of suicide attempts mirrors the national averages of women who have not needed the surgery, showing that it's not the surgery but the motivation behind it.

A recent study revealed that fifty-one percent of teenage males who identify as transgender have attempted suicide and thirty percent of females who struggle with gender identity have tried to take their life. At the risk of sounding politically incorrect, if they were changing to what they thought to be their true gender, wouldn't they feel better about themselves and not worse?

Where did this desire to change our appearance come from? Why are we so dissatisfied with our outward appearance? It goes back to the beginning of time. When Adam and Eve were in the garden of Eden, God said they could eat fruit from any tree except the tree of the knowledge of good and evil:

> Then the Lord God took the man and put him in the garden of Eden to tend and keep it. And the Lord God commanded the man, saying, "Of every tree of the garden you may freely eat; but of the tree of the knowledge of good and evil you shall

not eat, for in the day that you eat of it you shall surely die."
(Genesis 2: 15–17)

Adam and Eve lived a perfect life in the garden. They had food, they had each other, and they communed regularly with God. There was no sin in the world, and there was no shame:

And they were both naked, the man and his wife, and were not ashamed. (Genesis 2: 25)

Adam and Eve were tempted, ate the fruit, their eyes were opened, and they realized they were naked:

So when the woman saw that the tree was good for food, that it was pleasant to the eyes, and a tree desirable to make one wise, she took of its fruit and ate. She also gave to her husband with her, and he ate. Then the eyes of both of them were opened, and they knew that they were naked; and they sewed fig leaves together and made themselves coverings.
(Genesis 3: 6–7)

For the first time, they could see their outward appearance with the knowledge of evil and they were ashamed. That is part of the curse and a result of the fall. Man's eyes were opened at the fall, and every generation has had the knowledge of the presence of evil. Furthermore, every generation can see their outward appearance and are ashamed.

Jesus said the ability to see evil is actually a form of blindness:

Jesus heard that they had cast him out; and when He had found him, He said to him, "Do you believe in the Son of God?"

He answered and said, "Who is He, Lord, that I may believe in Him?"

And Jesus said to him, "You have both seen Him and it is He who is talking with you."

Then he said, "Lord, I believe!" And he worshiped Him.

And Jesus said, "For judgment I have come into this world, that those who do not see may see, and that those who see may be made blind."

Then some of the Pharisees who were with Him heard these words, and said to Him, "Are we blind also?"

Jesus said to them, "If you were blind, you would have no sin; but now you say, 'We see.' Therefore, your sin remains. (John 9:35–41)

Jesus had just healed the blind man. The Pharisees were so upset that they cast the healed man out of the Temple. Jesus heard about their ridiculous reaction and confronted them. He used the healing of the blind man as an analogy to show them that they were the ones who were really blind. He said because they could see evil, they were blind, but because the blind man could see good, He could truly see. This is another one of those opposite truths Jesus taught.

This wasn't the only time Jesus said that the Pharisees were blind. They weren't physically blind; He was talking about a spiritual blindness. The ability to see evil always results in spiritual blindness. He even said because they still see their sin, their sin remains. The Pharisees knew they weren't perfect, and that they knew because everyone's eyes were opened to see evil, others could see it in them. So, they covered it up by pretending to be good on the outside when they were evil on the inside:

> Woe to you, teachers of the law and Pharisees, you hypocrites! You clean the outside of the cup and dish, but inside they are full of greed and self-indulgence. Blind Pharisee! First clean the inside of the cup and dish, and then the outside also will be clean.

> Woe to you, teachers of the law and Pharisees, you hypocrites! You are like whitewashed tombs, which look beautiful on the outside but on the inside are full of the bones of the dead and everything unclean. In the same way, on the outside you appear to

people as righteous but, on the inside, you are full of hypocrisy and wickedness. (Matthew 23:25–28 NIV)

Jesus called them the "blind Pharisees." They were blind because they were concerned with outward appearance. They looked beautiful on the outside, but on the inside, they were full of death and everything unclean.

Isaiah 42:7 prophesied that Jesus came to open the eyes of the blind. This prophecy was for both the physical and spiritual healing of blindness. The Bible uses the phrase "their eyes were opened" several times. It was used to describe seeing good and bad. Adam and Eve's eyes were opened, and they could see evil and were ashamed. The Pharisees' eyes were opened, and they could see sin, so their sins remained. These are examples of seeing evil.

The disciples' eyes were opened, and they saw Jesus (Luke 24:31). The blind man's eyes were opened, and He regained his physical sight, but his spiritual eyes were also opened to see that Jesus was the Lord. These were examples of being able to see good

It confused me at first that the same phrase, "opened the eyes," was used to describe both the seeing of good and the seeing of evil until I realized that it's exactly what God said would happen when Adam and Eve ate the fruit. They ate from the tree of the knowledge of good and evil. It should not be a surprise that their eyes were opened so they could see good and they could also see evil. As a result, all of us are born with the ability to see good and evil. As it more directly applies to this book, we are all now born with the ability to see our outward appearance and all our flaws.

Jesus said the judgment is that those who see evil are really blind (John 9:39). For Adam and Eve, they were able to see their outward appearance, and it produced shame. Though they could see, they were really spiritually blind. When we look at outward appearance, we are looking through blind eyes. Just as Adam and Eve could see their outward appearance and were ashamed, when we look at our outward appearance, we're looking through blind eyes that produces shame in us.

That's why we're so obsessed with our appearance. When you look in the mirror and you're ashamed at your weight or anything else related to your appearance, you're looking through the blind eyes of the fall. When you get on the scales and you don't like what you see, you're looking through blind eyes. When you look at your body and are ashamed, you see yourself as a fallen person, not a person redeemed by Christ.

When your eyes are opened to the truth, you no longer see your outward appearance through blind eyes. You are no longer concerned about what you look like on the outside because you recognize who you are on the inside. In fact, those that truly see are those who can only see the good and are blind to the evil. When you reach that point, any need to lose weight or change your appearance becomes unimportant because you are focused on looking at your outward appearance through new eyes:

> Do not let your adornment be merely outward—arranging the hair, wearing gold, or putting on fine apparel— rather let it be the hidden person of the heart, with the incorruptible beauty of a gentle and quiet spirit, which is very precious in the sight of God. (1 Peter 3:3–4)

If you really saw yourself as Peter says you should in the above verse, you would not look at your outward appearance and be ashamed; you would only look at your inward beauty, which is precious in the sight of God. Do you really see yourself as incorruptibly beautiful? Do you see yourself as very precious in the sight of God? If you did, you would never get cosmetic surgery unless it was medically necessary.

All our plastic surgeries are nothing more than blind attempts to make our outward appearance look better because we see ourselves as fallen and we see the imperfections of the fall. Did you know that the most beautiful people in the world struggle with the same negative self-image? Why are models and beautiful actresses getting cosmetic surgeries? It's because they all see their bodies through the same blind eyes you see yours. They are part of the fall just like you are. They see their imperfections, and they are ashamed just like everyone else. That is why, after the surgery, you will still see an imperfection that you wish was changed. If you get to an ideal weight, you still won't be satisfied. The only way you will ever be satisfied is if you are able to look at yourself through opened spiritual eyes. Otherwise, you will be blind your whole life.

Diet plans, weight-loss plans, gym memberships, and plastic surgery all stem from the fact that we do not believe we are precious in the sight of God in our current physical condition.

So, what should be your weight-loss plan? You shouldn't have one. Don't spend one more minute concerned about your weight. Stay off the scales and quit looking at yourself in the mirror through fallen eyes. Look at yourself through the eyes of a redeemed person, not through the blind eyes of evil. When you do, the incorruptible beauty of a gentle and quiet spirit will be reflected in your outward appearance, and you will start to see dramatic changes in your physical appearance:

> As Jesus was speaking, one of the Pharisees invited him home for a meal. So, he went in and took his place at the table. His host was amazed to see that he sat down to eat without first performing the hand-washing ceremony required by Jewish custom. Then the Lord said to him, "You Pharisees are so careful to clean the outside of the cup and the dish, but inside you are filthy—full of greed and wickedness! Fools! Didn't God make the inside as well as the outside? So clean the inside by giving gifts to the poor, and you will be clean all over. (Luke 11:37–41 NLT)

Jesus said that what is on the inside will take over the outside. If you focus on the inside, your outward appearance will reflect the inward change. When you give thanks before each meal, you are changing what is on the inside. When you honor the body of Christ through the Lord's Supper, the food you eat is producing life in you. That is the only weight-loss plan you need. That food will produce life on the inside that will, in turn, produce life all over. You will lose weight. Your health will improve. It will happen through the work of God, not through your own self-effort.

JESUS DIET PRINCIPLE #8

Let God change you from the inside, and your outward appearance will change as well.

And then it will be a lasting change. You won't gain the weight back unless you start focusing on the wrong things again. If you let God use food to sculpt your body, it will be exactly like He wants it to be. And you will be beautiful inside and out.

This is a matter of changing what you see. Jesus gave you the opportunity to be redeemed from the curse. You still have the ability to see evil, but you can be blind to it. You still have the ability to see your physical imperfections, but you can see beyond them and into the spiritual.

When Paul was healed, the scales fell from his eyes, and he could see. In three days, Paul went from murdering Christians and hating Jesus to loving Him and becoming the author of two-thirds of the new testament. That is the type of transformation I have been hoping and praying you will receive. Today, you can start looking at your body through new eyes and thanking God for what He has done in your life.

You need the scales on your eyes to fall off to do that. It doesn't take God long to open spiritual eyes. When your eyes are open, you won't see the imperfections in your body. You won't wish you had different-colored eyes, a smaller nose, or bigger breasts. You will be perfectly satisfied with who you are in Christ.

If you have already had surgeries, don't worry about it, because you are under grace. However, I hope you see that you played right into the enemy's plan. He would like nothing more than for you to see yourself and your imperfections and be dissatisfied with who you are in Christ. It is not too late to have your eyes opened so you can see the truth.

This principle can apply to other areas of your life as well. When you are angry at your spouse, you are looking at him or her through fallen and blind eyes. You are seeing imperfections and not seeing him or her through spiritual eyes. When we judge one another, we are looking at them through the curse of the fall. We would not even have the capacity to see their faults if we didn't have the knowledge of good and evil. That knowledge creates the opportunity for us to look at every situation through blind eyes. If you only look at life through those blind eyes, you will live a life of emotional pain. Look at the anguish David was going through because of his sin:

> Because of your anger, my whole body is sick;
> my health is broken because of my sins.
> My guilt overwhelms me—
> it is a burden too heavy to bear.
> My wounds fester and stink
> because of my foolish sins.
> I am bent over and racked with pain.
> All day long I walk around filled with grief.
> A raging fever burns within me,
> and my health is broken.
> I am exhausted and completely crushed.
> My groans come from an anguished heart.
> (Psalm 38:3–8 NLT)

This is an example of someone who was looking through blind eyes. All he could see was his guilt. As a result, his body was sick, his health was broken, he was racked with pain, a fever burned within him, and he was completely exhausted and crushed.

David lived under the old covenant law of sin and death. He saw his life through the blind eyes of the fall. We live under the new covenant of grace. Your identity is in Christ if you know Him.

It's no wonder that weight-loss plans don't work. They can't when the motivation is to try to mask the shame from the fall. Of course, you regret plastic surgeries when you get one so-called imperfection fixed and then you see more every time you look in the mirror. It is no shock to me that a transgender boy or girl would want to end his or her life when they only see themselves through fallen and blind eyes.

Salvation is the opportunity to look at life through new eyes. You saw earlier that the Greek word for *salvation* is "sozo" which means wholeness. That is what Jesus wants for you. He will change you on the inside, and you will be changed all over.

CHAPTER 14
THE HUNGER GAMES

And Jesus said to them, "I am the bread of life. He who comes to Me
shall never hunger, and he who believes in Me shall never thirst.
(John 6:35)

The *Hunger Games* is a bizarre best-selling book and hit movie. More
than sixty-five million books have been sold, and four movies made
from the series. It's a televised competition in which children are
randomly chosen to fight to the death in a public arena. The winner
is lavished with riches, fame, and supplies for their home district.
The losers are left to struggle with very little food for another year.
The writer said her main inspiration was a story from Greek
mythology in which Minos forced Athens to sacrifice seven children
and seven maids to the Minotaur, who proceeds to kill them in a
labyrinth. While the book and movie are extremely popular, they
provide a very dark depiction of what man will do for food.

There are a number of bizarre real-life games played throughout
the world. These competitions are not for food but for competition's
sake. Have you ever heard of the Extreme Ironing Championship? I
can already tell you that my wife has no interest in ever playing that
game. She hates ironing with a passion, and it is one of her least favorite things to do. Extreme Ironing is a sport (if you can call it a
sport) where contestants take an ironing board and iron to extreme
locations and iron clothes. It is not without danger. Some locations

where extreme ironing has taken place include hanging from the side of a mountain, rock climbing, skiing or snowboarding, standing in the middle of a freeway, parachuting, under ice in a frozen lake, and underwater while scuba diving. The world record for underwater ironing is eighty-six divers all ironing underwater at the same time. I wonder how they kept from being electrocuted from the cord!

There's the World Worm Charming Championship. While it has never caught on in America, last year was its thirty-ninth year in Cheshire, England. Contestants are assigned a three-by-three plot of ground, and the winner is the person who can entice the most worms to the surface. The world record holder is a ten-year-old girl who charmed 567 worms to come to the surface. Don't ask me what you must do to charm that many worms. It was hard enough for me to charm one woman into marrying me, much less charm 567 worms!

Another English sport that has never caught on in America is the World Toe Wrestling Championship. Englishman Alan "Nasty" Nash has won it a record fifteen times. There's no way I'm locking toes with someone named Nasty! I would just forfeit. They have been trying for years to get this sport (although I use the word "sport," again, with hesitancy) into the Olympics. This is a serious sport in that many contestants have trainers and masseuses who travel with them. It is also dangerous. Nasty has dislocated his big toe nine times in competition. He just snaps the toe back in place, puts ice on it between rounds, and keeps going. He said in an interview his strategy is that in the first round of the competition, he tries to hurt the other person so badly that everyone else is afraid of him the rest of the competition. And they take it very seriously. There is a thick rulebook you have to follow, and if you don't toe the line, you will be disqualified.

There is chess boxing. It goes for eleven rounds, and every other round, they alternate between boxing and chess. You can win by either knockout or checkmate. They say the quality of chess goes down as the fight wears on. That's not surprising. I would think that blows to the head tend to make it harder to plan your chess moves.

There is the World Shin Kicking Contest, which is also held in England. What is it with the British? There is no doubt that the American Revolution was a good thing. I much prefer baseball, football, and basketball to extreme ironing, toe wrestling and shin kicking! Shin kicking contests have been going on in Cotswold, England, for more than four hundred years. The Rock-Paper-Scissors World Championship was started in America in 2002. That sounds more like something Americans would come up with and is much safer than toe wrestling and shin kicking. It is popular in the states and has even been nationally televised. I don't think it will ever become America's pastime, however.

We all know about horse racing and dog racing. Did you know about camel and ostrich racing? There is also cockroach racing which started in 1982 in Australia. There's the World Snail Racing Championship. That doesn't seem like very compelling television either. The world record has been held since 1995 by Archie, who went thirteen inches in less than two minutes. Last year's winner, Herbie 2, only traveled the course in three minutes and twenty-five seconds. I guess snails aren't as athletic as they used to be. Man is getting faster as time goes on, but snails must be getting lazier because they are getting slower.

There is the wife carrying race. A man carries a woman through an extreme obstacle course filled with hazards. The couple who completes the course in the fastest time wins. I learned you don't actually have to be married to participate. Not sure why it is called the World Wife Carrying Championship. My wife has no interest in that contest, and neither do I.

There are a number of world championship kissing contests. I can't get my wife interested in those either. You actually don't have to be married to compete in them. The world record for the longest kiss was set by a couple from Thailand. They locked lips for fifty-eight hours, thirty-five minutes, and fifty-eight seconds. I love my wife, and she is a great kisser, but I don't want to kiss her for fifty-eight hours! They have very strict rules to qualify for a world record. Their lips must be touching at all times, the couple must be awake and standing at all times, they can't be propped up by anything or anyone, no rest breaks are allowed, and no adult diapers are permitted. Not sure how they handle the restroom issues, and I honestly don't want to know! I guess the breath issues aren't a problem either.

There is the hairiest back competition. Probably too much information, but I wouldn't do well in that competition. There is the World Beard and Moustache Championship. I wouldn't do very well in that competition either. I can't grow a beard or a mustache that looks good at all. There is the World's Ugliest Dog Championship and the World Air Guitar Championships. I had no idea how many people are into air guitars. Literally tens of thousands of people in dozens of countries around the world participate in various levels of competition until they reach the annual world championships. The winners are actually listed by year in Wikipedia.

I'm not sure why but eating the most food has become a competition. Joey Chestnut is the world hot dog eating champion. This past year, he set a world record eating seventy-four hog dogs in ten minutes. He holds a number of other championships and world records. He has eaten 141 hard-boiled eggs in eight minutes, seventy bratwursts in ten minutes, and seventy-eight matzoh balls in eight minutes. He scarfed down 4.5 pounds of steak plus sides in nine minutes. He gorged down 13.76 pounds of pork ribs in twelve minutes and 12.8 pounds of asparagus in ten minutes. Before you decide that he's crazy, you should know he has made as much as $500,000 in one year from prize money and sponsorships! He is crazy, by the way, and there are much better ways to make a living.

Joey Chestnut doesn't eat because he is hungry. Neither do most Americans. Only one in six Americans is at their ideal weight. The reason is that we eat more food than God intended for us to eat.

God gave us hunger so that we would know when to eat and how much to eat. There is nothing wrong with hunger. Hunger is our body telling us that it needs fuel. The Greek word for "hunger" in the Bible means to need food. The problem is that we don't just eat when we need food; we eat when we don't need food and that's why we're overweight. Jesus showed us the proper relationship we are to have with food when He fed the multitude:

> Now Jesus called His disciples to Himself and said, "I have compassion on the multitude, because they have now continued with Me three days and have nothing to eat. And I do not want to send them away hungry, lest they faint on the way."
> (Matthew 15:32)

> So, He commanded the multitude to sit down on the ground. And He took the seven loaves and the fish and gave thanks, broke them and gave them to His disciples; and the disciples gave to the multitude. So they all ate and were filled, and they took up seven large baskets full of the fragments that were left.
> (Matthew 15:35–37)

Jesus said He did not want them to be hungry. God does not want us to be hungry. The multitude had been with Jesus, listening to His teachings for three whole days. Today, when we go to a concert or a sporting event, there are food vendors everywhere. We always have plenty of food, but there were no food vendors out in the area where Jesus was preaching. The Bible doesn't say, but I wonder if they had eaten anything over the three days. They certainly would not have brought enough food with them to last for three days. The throngs always just rushed to see Jesus whenever He came to their area. There were more than four thousand men, not including women and children, who were there those days.

The people were hanging on every word and probably weren't even thinking about food. I wonder if they were so enthralled with

Jesus that they didn't even notice they weren't eating. Perhaps they went into town and ate and then came back. We don't really know. All we know is that after three days, they were so hungry Jesus was concerned they would faint on the way home. My guess is they hadn't eaten anything. Jesus said He did not want to send them away hungry. God created us to be hungry when we needed food, and He doesn't want us to ever go hungry for very long.

They only had seven loaves and two fishes. The disciples said they didn't have enough money to feed everyone, so Jesus told them to sit down and He would take care of it. He multiplied the food, and the Bible says they all ate until they were "filled." God wants us to eat until we are filled. There is nothing wrong with eating when you are hungry and eating until you are full. Notice there were seven baskets full of leftovers. They didn't eat all the food that was available; they just ate what they needed, to be full, and they left the rest.

Here is the next principle of the Jesus Diet that Jesus modeled for us:

JESUS DIET PRINCIPLE #9
Eat when you are hungry; quit when you are full.

Jesus got hungry. Jesus was going to Jerusalem from Bethany, and the Bible says He became hungry (Mark 11:12). When Jesus was fasting in the wilderness for forty days, the Bible says: "Afterwards, He became hungry." It is interesting that Jesus wasn't hungry for the forty days. He became hungry after the fast was over.

When Jesus met the woman at the well, He asked her for a drink. He was just like us in that regard. He got hungry and thirsty just like we get hungry and thirsty. The religious leaders even lied about Jesus and tried to make him out to be a glutton and a drunkard:

The Son of Man came eating and drinking, and you say, 'Here is a **glutton** and a **drunkard**, a friend of tax collectors and sinners.'

(Luke 7:34 NIV) (Emphasis Added)

Jesus was accused of being a glutton and a drunkard! It was a false accusation. The Bible says gluttony and drunkenness are sins. Gluttony is eating more food than you need, and drunkenness is drinking alcohol to excess. We know Jesus never sinned, so He never overate and never drank too much wine. The Bible even says that gluttony and drunkenness are associated with idolatry:

> "Neither be ye **idolaters**, as were some of them; as it is written, "The people sat down to eat and drink, and rose up to play." (1 Corinthians 10:7 KJV) (Emphasis Added)

Overindulging in food and alcohol is idolatry because, when we overeat and overdrink, we are controlled by our own flesh and not by the Spirit of God. Read Philippians 3:19 (NIV):

> Their destiny is destruction, their **god** is their **stomach**, and their glory is in their shame. Their mind is set on earthly things. (Emphasis Added)

Their god is their stomach! That is what we have done today: we have made our god our stomachs. Satisfying our flesh with food and drink has become our god. We don't intend for it to be idolatry, but it is. We would never make an idol and worship it, but we will indulge our flesh to the point we eat more food than our bodies need, and then we are overweight, which leads to all kinds of health problems. We eat more food than we need, and we drink more than we need to satisfy our flesh. We don't eat because we are hungry and need food; we eat to satisfy our stomachs. That's why the Bible says our stomachs have become our god. We are controlled by our stomachs. When we are controlled by something other than God, that thing becomes an idol for us. Idolatry is defined as the worship of a false god.

And we don't need to overeat. If we just ate when we were hungry and stopped when we were full and left the rest, we would get to our ideal weight within a short period of time. Anyone who is over-weight is so because they eat more food than they need. Paul said that he had learned to be content in whatever situation he found himself:

I know what it is to be in need, and I know what it is to have plenty. I have learned the secret of being **content** in any and every situation, whether **well fed or hungry**, whether living in plenty or in want. (Philippians 4:12 NIV) (Emphasis Added)

Whether he was well fed or hungry, Paul learned to be content. Jesus said that if we followed after Him, we would never be hungry or thirsty:

Do not work for food that spoils, but for food that endures to eternal life, which the Son of Man will give you. For on him God the Father has placed his seal of approval. (John 6:27 NIV)

Then Jesus declared, "I am the bread of life. Whoever comes to me will never go hungry, and whoever believes in me will never be thirsty. (John 6:35 NIV)

Jesus was speaking in a metaphor. He said to not seek after food that spoils and only satisfies for a moment, but to seek after Him. He is the Bread of Life. If we seek after Him and come to Him, we will never be hungry, and if we believe in Him, we will never be thirsty. Even though He is speaking in a metaphor, I believe this has earthly meaning as well. Jesus said He will give us this eternal food. Jesus also said God would give us whatever earthly food we needed:

Look at the birds of the air, for they neither sow nor reap nor gather into barns; yet your heavenly Father feeds them. Are you not of more value than they? (Matthew 6:26)

We will never hunger or thirst for an eternity, and it starts the moment we believe in Jesus. We will never hunger or thirst for food or drink on this earth! This doesn't mean we will never be hungry or thirsty, but rather that God will always supply the food to satisfy our hunger and the drink to satisfy our thirst. Have you ever seen an overweight bird? The birds of the air always have enough food. God doesn't give them more than what they need; He gives them just the right amount that they need to live. They have more food than they need available to them. There is no limit to the number of worms they can eat each day. The birds instinctively know how much to eat and when to quit eating.

John 6:27 says Jesus will give us this food. He actually said He is that food. We saw in the Lord's Supper that He is the bread that is broken for us. Jesus will supply all of our eternal needs and all of our earthly needs, including food and water through His broken body. Why? Because we are way more valuable than the birds.

God is not going to supply more than we need, because that's gluttony. Whatever we eat that is more than we need is from our own self-indulgence and not from God. Jesus is all that we need. Jesus is everything we need to sustain our life.

What you will find is that you don't have to control your eating by self-effort. When you first begin the Jesus Diet and start giving thanks for your food before you eat it and begin to properly discern the body of Christ, an amazing thing will happen: your cravings for food will go away. I used to get hungry every two hours because I was eating all the time. I generally chose foods that were healthier than the alternatives, but I found myself constantly wanting to eat. There is even a diet that says to eat six to eight small meals a day. I had heard of that diet and loosely followed it. It purports that eating every two to three hours keeps you from overeating. That didn't work for me because I found myself gaining weight.

The Jesus Diet changed everything for me. When I started giving thanks for my food before I ate it and when I discerned properly the body of Christ, not only did the food begin the process of healing my body of every sickness and disease, but the food satisfied me in a way that it hadn't before. Jesus said in John 6:35 that if we seek Him first, then we will never be hungry or thirsty. It is not that I am not ever hungry or thirsty, because I am, rather; when I eat and drink, giving thanks and with discernment of the body of Christ, the food satisfies my hunger and thirst.

You may be thinking, "I'm hungry all the time!" That is not how God designed your body. Your body is designed to give you the feeling of hunger whenever your body needs food for fuel. When you are feeling hungry even though your body doesn't need food, then that is simply your flesh craving something that is not from God. It is really your mind and body tricking you into thinking you are hungry. I know it feels like you are hungry, but you are really not.

I read a number of interesting studies related to hunger and food and how the mind works. Brian Wansick won a Nobel prize for a study that measured the fullness of subjects who ate bowls of soup. One group was given a bowl of soup with a tube on the bottom that kept a steady supply of soup in the bowl. The eaters did not realize that the bowl was slowly refilling itself, and they ate seventy-three percent more soup than those who were just given a bowl of soup that didn't refill itself. At the end of the study, the ones who ate from the self-filling bowls did not rate themselves any fuller than the ones who ate from the normal bowls. It was all an illusion. The amount they ate was not what was important. What made them full was the amount they thought they were eating.

A study was conducted with apples. One group of people ate an apple, and another group simply smelled the apples. Both groups felt full. Sniffing the apple tricked the brain into thinking it was actually eating the food. The hunger went away because the brain thought it had eaten an apple.

It has been proven that if you eat foods that take longer to chew, then you become full faster. If you eat foods that have more fiber, your stomach feels full faster, and the hunger pains go away. It's not the amount of food you are eating that satisfies the hunger; it is your mind thinking you have eaten the right amount of food to satisfy the hunger.

What we can learn from these studies is that hunger is not always real, or at least it is not necessarily an accurate gauge of what your body needs. It is definitely a feeling that seems real, but it is not necessarily based on reality. Just because you feel hunger does not necessarily mean that you are hungry and need food. Just because you don't feel hunger doesn't mean that you don't need food.

Individuals who go on a fast notice that after a couple of days, the hunger pangs go away completely. In a spiritual fast, the hunger in the flesh is giving way to the Spirit. If you are just fasting, your mind gives up after a while and quits making you feel hungry. Smokers trying to quit are told to endure the craving for a cigarette for fifteen minutes and that the craving will then go away. Eventually, the cravings will go away completely, and the smokers will wean themselves off cigarettes. The point is that you are not slaves to your cravings, and they are not your gods. You can resist them.

But really, you don't even have to do it on your own, because Jesus does it for you. Just give thanks before you eat your food and look at every meal as the Lord's Supper, discerning the body of Christ, and the food you eat will satisfy you. The hunger pains will go away, and you will find yourself going much longer periods of time without feeling hungry.

If that doesn't happen, then there may be some physical reason why you are feeling hungry when you don't really need food. Thyroid issues can affect hunger. Hormonal issues, anxiety, depression, and stress can trigger overeating. Habits can affect how much you eat. Eating in front of the television or while driving a car can distract you to the point that you don't realize how much you are eating, and before you know it, you have eaten more than you need. Portion size obviously affects how much we eat. We tend to eat whatever is put in front of us.

My wife and I started ordering one meal at restaurants instead of two. We share the meal, so we are eating half as much. Our brains are wired to eat whatever portion is in front of us, and we generally feel full as soon as we finish the portion. The portion size doesn't really affect whether we are full or not after we eat it. We are full either way once we finish the portion that is in front of us. We decided that we might as well eat the smaller portion if that is all the food we need. And we save money as an added benefit.

We eat three meals a day at the same time because we have programmed ourselves to eat at those times. We might not necessarily be hungry, but we eat, nonetheless. Eating when you are hungry helps you to develop a new routine, and you will find yourself eating less.

If you eat candy that is in a wrapper, studies have shown that you eat thirty percent less. When you have to work to get it open, it takes longer to eat, and you get full faster. If you drink a glass of water before you eat, your stomach doesn't recognize whether it is full of drinking water or full of food. It thinks it is full, and the hunger goes away.

There are thousands of practical suggestions for eating less. There is nothing wrong with thinking about them and implementing them. I am mostly saying that you don't have to do any of those things. When you begin following the Jesus Diet and thanking God for your food before every meal, discerning the body of Christ, Jesus does it for you. You will become content with what you eat and what you drink, and you will see real change. You will reach your ideal weight within a reasonable period of time. Just be mindful of what Jesus is doing inside of you. He is changing you. The food is changing you. I have fasted many times over the years. When I first began the Jesus Diet, I noticed I had the same feelings inside that I have when I am fasting. When I'm fasting, I feel closer to God, and I feel a physical change as well. I feel cleaner inside. It's hard to describe if you have never felt it. It feels to me like the fast is cleansing my body of toxins and there is an overwhelming sense of well-being. I feel that way most of the time now on the Jesus Diet. I don't overeat, and I don't even notice it. The spiritual benefits are the most important thing. The physical benefits are the bonus.

That's not to say that you can't ever overeat or that you always deny yourself food. God commanded the children of Israel to set aside certain times of the year to have "feasts." They would gather together and have huge feasts celebrating what God had done for them. Notice what God told them to do in Deuteronomy 14:24–26:

> When the Lord your God has blessed you, then you shall exchange it for money, take the money in your hand, and go to the place which the Lord your God chooses. And you shall spend that money for whatever your heart desires: for oxen or sheep, for wine or similar drink, for whatever your heart desires; you shall eat there before the Lord your God, and you shall rejoice, you and your household.

When God has blessed you, take some money and go get food and whatever you want to drink, whatever your heart desires, and eat it there and rejoice! Eat as much as you want and drink the beverage of your choice. By the way, don't let anyone tell you that you can't drink alcohol. The Bible never forbids it. Jesus drank wine. The Lord's Supper was taken with wine. Paul said to Timothy to take wine for his stomach. We don't live under laws anymore. Any attempt by man to create a law puts you back under a system of sin and death. You have been set free from the law of sin and death.

I rarely drink alcohol. That's because I don't like the taste and I figured early on that if I never drank, I would never have a problem. Alcohol has destroyed many people's lives, but God does not forbid it altogether. I don't judge anyone who drinks it; just don't drink too much. Just don't eat too much as well. If that is how you generally live your life, then there will be times when you can have a feast. Just don't eat like that and drink like that every day. You will end up weak, sick, and dying prematurely. You will end up overweight, an alcoholic, or worse.

On the Jesus Diet, physical healing manifested in my body when

I started giving thanks before each meal and discerning the body of Christ. I needed reading glasses for the past fifteen years. I was always looking for glasses, so I went to the Dollar Store and bought ten or so pairs. I put them all around the house so I would always have a pair within reach. When I preached, I couldn't see the Scriptures without my reading glasses. I was constantly taking them on and off. One day, I noticed I was reading something and didn't need my glasses! I was completely healed. The Bible says that Moses died when he was 120 years old and his eyes had not dimmed!

I cannot express enough how dramatic the change is once you start the Jesus Diet. Try it for yourself. It will change your life. Not the diet, not this book, and not my ideas. Jesus will change you. Jesus will heal you. Jesus will satisfy your hunger. Jesus will break your addiction to food or to alcohol. You don't have to do it on your own; He will do it for you. What is Your part?

Then they asked him, "What must we do to do the works God requires?"

Jesus answered, "The work of God is this: to believe in the one he has sent." (John 6:28–29 NIV)

Your part is to believe! That's the only work that you must do, and Jesus will do the rest. Get rid of your diet plans and get rid of your self-efforts. Resist the devil's attempts to get you back under the law. Quit feeling guilty because you are overweight. Quit feeling shame and condemnation. There is no condemnation for those who are in Christ Jesus. Gluttony and drunkenness are not unpardonable sins. You are forgiven for them. Just let Jesus do His work of restoration in your body.

Let Jesus satisfy your hunger, and you will never go hungry again. Just believe that if you give thanks before every meal and you discern the body of Christ, you will be healed. Eat when you are hungry and stop when you are full, and you will get to your ideal weight. You will start to eat the foods you need to live. Your cravings will go away, and you will be set free. Just believe. Tomorrow, we are going to look at the role physical exercise should play in your health.

CHAPTER 15
NO PAIN, JUST GAIN

For what will it profit a man if he gains the whole world, and loses his own soul? (Mark 8:36)

I have owned my own businesses for almost forty years. Warren Buffett, one of the greatest entrepreneurs and investors of all time, said there are two rules to investing and business. Rule number one is don't lose money. Rule number two is never forget rule number one. A business must make a profit if it is going to stay in business for very long. A business makes a profit when its income exceeds its expenses. When expenses exceed its income, it has a loss.

There have been many strange businesses that have surprisingly made a profit. In 1975, a man had the idea to take stones from Rosarita Beach in Mexico and sell them as pet rocks. They were marketed like live pets in a box with straw and breathing holes. The idea was that a rock did not have to be fed, watered, bathed, or groomed and was the perfect pet. Of course, anyone could have gone outside in their backyard and adopted any rock as a pet, but this idea sold 1.5 million rocks at four dollars each, helping the entrepreneur become a millionaire in the process. The rocks were basically free except for the labor to gather them, and straw was very cheap, so the only real cost was the box and marketing. It was a very profitable venture, however, the founder was harassed with lawsuits and threats. In 1988 he said: "Sometimes, I look back and wonder if my life would have been simpler if I hadn't done it."

A Canadian company sells Air-in-a-Can. They take air from the Colorado mountains, bottle it, and sell it to people in China who live in smog infested areas. It started out as a joke on eBay and turned into a profitable business as demand has grown. I'm not sure why anyone would buy air that is free, but we also buy bottled water every day even though water is free. I'll just stick to the air God gave me.

Speaking of what God gave me, another company is selling spots in heaven. For $12.99 plus shipping, you can purchase insurance guaranteeing you'll get into heaven. It comes with a certificate, ID card, and an informational guide with directions on how to get there. It also comes with a money-back guarantee. If you don't make it to heaven, they will fully refund your money! I wonder how exactly you collect it.

A company in Japan offers an apology service. If you need or want to apologize to someone, you hire this company, and they will apologize on your behalf. They will write a letter of apology, or if you are willing to pay more, the apology can be in person. Somehow, I don't think my wife would accept my apology if it were coming from a company I'd paid to apologize for me. How genuine could that apology be? It also occurs to me that I know some people who don't have enough money to cover everyone who deserves an apology from them!

Have you ever heard of Chia Pets? Another crazy idea that has sold more than 500,000 units a year since the early 1980s. It is a figurine that sprouts "hair" from chia sprouts. Today, there are chia playing cards, chia alarm clocks, chia watches, and chia flower gardens. Personally, I think they are weird looking, but apparently, they're also a good business idea.

Even more bizarre is the Big Mouth Billy Bass. One of those was hanging on my aunt's wall in the living room. It's a bass mounted on a piece of decorative wood that sings on cue. It turns its head and tail towards you and belts out a tune like "I Will Survive," the Gloria Gaynor hit song. There is now a deer, bear, and even a lobster version. The holiday fish comes complete with a Santa's hat and a sleigh bell on its tail. Jeff Foxworthy famously said that if you own more than three of these, you might be a redneck. I think some members of my family qualify.

Here is an idea that didn't catch on. Do you ever find yourself needing a quarter and can't find one? It happens all the time. You need a quarter for the laundromat, parking meter, or drive-through window and one is nowhere to be found when you need it. One company came up with a solution. They'll sell you a package of twenty dollars in quarters for twenty-seven dollars! How dumb do they think we are?

The most ridiculous business idea I heard was the man who authored a book filled with two hundred blank pages. He has sold more than 100,000 copies. The book has been translated into nine languages. I doubt he has sold the movie rights. I'm not sure anyone would go to that movie. For that matter, I'm not sure why anyone would buy the book. I'm glad I didn't think of it. Amazon has banned the book on their website. I don't condone censorship, but good for them.

Jesus spoke a lot about profit. He used several parables about money and finances to make spiritual points. He was concerned that our lives would be profitable, not so much from a financial sense but from a spiritual sense. He said it is not profitable for you to gain the world but lose your soul (Mark 8:36). He was talking about the pursuit of worldly things over the pursuit of things that matter in eternity.

The inventor (and I use the term loosely) of the Pet Rock realized that worldly profits are not always very fulfilling. While the Pet Rock made him a millionaire, he wondered if it was really worth the effort. So many things in life that are pursued through the works of the flesh or in obedience to the law are just not worth the effort. I try and focus my life on those things that actually profit me.

JESUS DIET PRINCIPLE #10
Pursue those things that really profit you.

For instance, on the Jesus Diet, you are free to eat and drink anything you want under the direction of the Holy Spirit. All foods are clean, and all drinks are allowed. Gluttony and drunkenness are sins, but they are not the unpardonable sin. You can eat too much and drink in excess and still get to heaven. But what will it profit you on this earth? The result of gluttony is obesity, sickness, and disease. The result of drunkenness is alcoholism, broken relationships, and, ultimately, liver disease.

Everyone is faced with this decision: are you going to pursue the desires of your flesh and spend most of your life indulging them, or are you going to pursue those things that will actually profit you? James 1:15 says sin comes from our desires. When desire is conceived, it gives birth to sin, and when sin is full-grown, it brings forth death. For those in Christ, it is not eternal death, but sin produces death here on earth: death of dreams, death of marriages, death of relationships and businesses, and sometimes even physical death if the sin is grievous enough.

You are free from the law of sin and death, but what does that mean for the believer. You are no longer bound to follow a set of rules and regulations. You are perfectly free to indulge in whatever sinful activity you want, including overeating and drunkenness. The result will be health problems, broken relationships, and death. Paul addressed this in Galatians 5:13 (NIV):

> You, my brothers and sisters, were called to be free. But do not use your freedom to indulge the flesh; rather, serve one another humbly in love.

I spent the first chapters of this book trying to help you get free from the law of sin and death. I believe that most Christians are stuck in a mixture of grace and the law. We know we are forgiven for our sins, but we still live in the law as if we aren't really forgiven. Our churches preach a mixture of salvation by grace through faith, but you had better live a godly life, or God is going to punish you. We are told that if we sin, bad things are going to happen to us. And they do, but not because God is punishing you. There are always consequences to sin. Sin will never profit you, but sin comes from the law. We would not even be aware of our sin if not for the law (Romans 7:7). When the law came, sin actually increased (Romans 5:20). As people became more aware of their sin, they sinned more. This was not because the law was bad, but because man became sin conscious. The more he became aware of sin, the more he wanted to sin.

I want to be extremely careful how I present this chapter because Jesus came to set us free from that cycle of sin and punishment and I don't want to write a mixture of grace that will cause anyone to think they need to follow a certain dietary lifestyle in order to be healthy. It doesn't happen that way. At the same time, freedom doesn't mean we should indulge the flesh and just sin all the time. That does not profit us. It doesn't profit us to try and build a set of dietary and exercise laws in order to change our health through self-effort, nor does it profit us to indulge the flesh without limits.

I see two different extremes. There are those who don't restrict their eating or their drinking at all. Consequently, they are obese and/or become alcoholics. For the most part, they live a life of misery and trouble. Their behavior is of no profit to them. On the other extreme, I see those who focus so much on body image, exercise, diet, and health that it consumes their lives. Some do it out of vanity. They want to look good on the outside and impress their friends with their physique and look good in a bathing suit. There are individuals whose lives are consumed with running, exercise, and weight training, and they neglect their spouses, children, and church and focus their energies on something temporal. It is indulging the flesh just as much as overeating and drunkenness are.

Most people are in the middle. They go back and forth between dieting and indulging the flesh. Sometimes, they go through phases when they exercise regularly. Then they go through periods of time when they don't exercise for whatever reason. Generally, they feel guilty and try to get back into it, but it usually doesn't last.

Here is what Paul said about physical exercise:

For bodily exercise profiteth little: but godliness is profitable unto all things, having promise of the life that now is, and of that which is to come. (1 Timothy 4:8 KJV)

There is that word "profit" again. Bodily exercise is of some profit, but it's minimal. On the other hand, godliness is profitable unto all things. Notice that it's profitable not only for the life to come, but godliness is profitable for right now. You need to understand godliness. Paul is not talking about works. He is not talking about adherence to the law. We think being godly is being God-like. We think being godly is being holy and following the law perfectly. The Greek word for "godliness" actually means "devotion." In Titus 1, Paul says to "pursue" godliness. You are to pursue your devotion to God. The stem word for "godliness" also means to step back from. Godliness is to step back from the pursuit of worldly desires and our flesh and turn our focus to devotion to God.

I'm absolutely convinced that this is the way to live a "godly" life. It is not the strict adherence to the law. It is the pursuit of your devotion to God. If you really love God, you will not carry out the desires of your flesh, not because you have the ability on your own strength to overcome the flesh by keeping the law, but because your desires change, and you want to live a certain lifestyle out of devotion to God. I don't just stay faithful to my wife because the Bible says I should. I am faithful to my wife because of my devotion to her. I don't eat and drink a certain way because of some law, or even because I want to try to be healthy. My lifestyle is based on my devotion to God and my desire to serve Him with my body. I believe the best way to serve Him over a long period of time, is to be healthy. However, I discovered in the Jesus Diet that health comes through God working in me, not me doing it through self-effort.

On the Jesus Diet, your desire for food will change as your devotion to God changes. As your desire for food changes, your body will change. You will lose weight, you will grow stronger, your health problems will resolve themselves, your energy and vitality will increase, and your body image will be transformed. It won't be through your own self-effort but through the work of God in your life. I am going to make two seemingly contradictory statements: you need to be as healthy as possible in order to carry out God's plan for your life, and you will not achieve health through diet and exercise.

That concept is counterintuitive. The world tells you that you need to exercise in order to be fit. The world tells you that you need to go on a diet to lose weight. No! You need to pursue God. You need to pursue devotion to God. That is what will profit you, and that is what will change your life. That is what will transform your health.

How will it transform your health? The food you eat that is consecrated by God and eaten with thanksgiving will provide your body with the vitamins and minerals it needs to be healthy. The Lord's Supper taken with each meal will make you strong and healthy and give you a long life. You must turn your focus away from the food and exercise and turn your focus and devotion to God, and your health will be transformed. Your body will change. You will look good in your swimsuit, not because you were trying to look good for others or because you somehow managed to stick to a diet or exercise program, but because you don't care as much about what you look like on the outside. All you care about is being who

God wants you to be on the inside, and the outside will reflect the transformation.

And you will be healthier and stronger than you would be if you followed the exercise programs and diets. Look at what happened to Paul:

> Then some Jews came from Antioch and Iconium and won the crowd over. They stoned Paul and dragged him outside the city, thinking he was dead. But after the disciples had gathered around him, he got up and went back into the city. The next day he and Barnabas left for Derbe. (Acts 14:19–20 NIV)

Paul was preaching the gospel, and the crowd got so upset that they stoned him to the point where they thought he was dead. There were a number of ways in which a person was stoned to death in Paul's day. Generally, a person's hands were tied behind their back, and rocks were thrown. Sometimes the person was placed in a hole. In that instance, a man would be buried up to his waist, and a woman up to her breasts. Stones were thrown one at a time until the person was dead. If they were particularly cruel, they took their time to cause maximum suffering and torture. When a mob was acting on the spur of the moment, they often just surrounded the person and began to mercilessly pound them with rocks thrown by everyone at once. Sometimes, people were stoned by just one large boulder thrown onto their back or chest, crushing their internal organs and often killing the person instantly.

We don't know how Paul was stoned, but the crowd thought he was so badly injured that he was dead. The disciples gathered around him, and he got up! The next day, Paul walked to Derbe, which was thirty miles from Lystra. Paul walked thirty miles the day after being stoned to death or near death. How did he have the strength? Remember, Paul said physical exercise is of very little profit. His life was obviously not consumed by his exercise routine. He did not prepare for that day by physical training. An athlete who wants to run a marathon, trains for weeks. The more they train, the better prepared they are physically and mentally.

Paul found the strength through his devotion to God. He was strong physically because he was strong spiritually. He also needed God's divine intervention, or he would have likely died. When the disciples gathered around him, I am sure they laid hands on him, and God healed him. Paul stood right up! He could not have done that without divine intervention from God. When God healed him, he was completely healed. He must have had no side effects from the stoning. That is called divine health. It is health that is supernatural. Health that we create through diet and exercise is natural health. Health that comes from God is divine health. I want divine health.

Paul had no problem walking thirty miles the next day. In Paul's first missionary journey, he traveled more than 1200 miles. No amount of physical exercise and training would have prepared Paul for the rigors of his journeys. Many of those miles were walked. Many of those trips were filled with physical abuse and persecution.

How did Paul maintain his health through the duration of those trips? He said thanks before he took a meal, he discerned properly the body of Christ in the taking of the Lord's Supper, and he was strong and healthy enough to endure whatever he faced and to fulfill God's plan for his life. His daily thanksgiving for food and his discernment of the body of Christ profited him greatly. He was physically and spiritually prepared for anything. And he had to be:

> The crowd joined in the attack against Paul and Silas, and the magistrates ordered them to be stripped and beaten with rods. After they had been severely flogged, they were thrown into prison, and the jailer was commanded to guard them carefully. When he received these orders, he put them in the inner cell and fastened their feet in the stocks.

> About midnight Paul and Silas were praying and singing hymns to God, and the other prisoners were listening to them.
> (Acts 16: 22–25 NIV)

Paul and Silas were "severely flogged." It says they were beaten with rods. Rods were either smooth or prickly. Either one inflicted tremendous punishment, and damage to the body. In the Histories of Saints Hermillus and Stratonicus, the writer documented what it was like to be beaten with rods during the time of Paul:

> Greatly angered at these words, Licinus ordered Stratonicus to be stretched face upward and thrashed on the stomach with rods of a three-cornered shape. Now this was a grievous torture, scarcely tolerable by the human frame, for the corners of these rods cruelly cut the flesh like so many swords.

Paul and Silas were severely flogged and thrown into prison. No one took care of their wounds. No one fed them or gave them anything to drink. They were actually put into stocks binding their hands and feet, so they couldn't tend to their wounds at all. My wife and I were in Rome recently and visited one of the prisons where Paul and Peter were held. The prison cells were actually underground and essentially a cave. They were in good shape for the tours, but I can imagine that in those days, they were a filthy mess. The unsanitary conditions must have been almost unbearable. With open wounds like Paul and Silas must have suffered, the threat of infection would have to have been high. With the loss of blood, nothing to dull the pain, and no food or drink to give them strength, they were probably near death again.

What were Paul and Silas doing? They were praising God and singing hymns. What a powerful representation of their devotion to God. God responded by causing an earthquake that immediately freed them from their chains. The Bible says nothing about them praying and asking God to get them out of the prison. They were simply expressing their devotion to God, and God responded with deliverance and healing:

> Then they spoke the word of the Lord to him and to all who were in his house. And he took them the same hour of the night and

washed their stripes. And immediately he and all his family were baptized. Now when he had brought them into his house, he set food before them; and he rejoiced, having believed in God with all his household. (Acts 16: 32–34)

Even the jailer was saved. Their singing and praising God under those circumstances must have significantly impacted the jailer. I'm sure he couldn't believe they were so joyful in the midst of so much suffering. God then used the jailer to bring healing to their bodies. He took them to his house, treated their wounds, and gave them something to eat and drink. It doesn't say, but I'm sure Paul gave thanks before he ate anything.

The next day, Paul and Silas went to the next town. How did they do that? They were severely beaten the day before. They went back to work the next day. Most of us would have been off work for weeks. Where did they get the strength? It was a free gift of grace. There's no way they could have recovered that fast on their own. There is no doctor today who could have had them back on their feet that quickly. Only God could do it. Only God could give them divine health.

That is what I want for you. You may not be beaten with rods or stoned to within an inch of your life, but you face your own challenges. You can get weary from the stress of just living your life. Most people are not in the physical condition to withstand anything like what Paul went through. Fortunately, you don't have to be. We face our own challenges; they are just different from what Paul faced. However, most Christians are not in the physical condition to withstand even the things life throws at us now.

That's why you get sick so easily. That is why you get depressed and anxious so often. The average adult gets two to four colds a year, and the average child gets eight to twelve colds a year. Most Christians' bodies are not prepared to resist cancer, diabetes, heart disease, and all manner of sickness we face today. We think it's because we eat the wrong foods and don't exercise enough. That is what we have been told. We have spent years feeling guilty about it. It is not because we don't eat right, and it's not because we don't exercise enough. It is because we are not devoted to God in a way that brings about divine health.

When difficult circumstances come upon us, we don't immediately praise God and sing hymns. We are worried and anxiously blame God or others for our trouble. When we are sick, our first response is to run to the doctor hoping he will prescribe a drug that will mask the symptoms. Rather than turning to God in devotion, we often blame God for not healing us and get mad at Him for not immediately fixing our circumstances, or we beg God, crying out to Him, hoping our tears will move Him to act.

We don't realize that God is always there, ready to restore. That's His nature. Those are His promises to us. Paul never worried about it. He preached the gospel with boldness, not caring for his life. Paul didn't worry if he was thrown in prison. He praised God anyway. He was so devoted to God that he barely noticed his wounds. If he was wounded, he believed God would heal him. I wouldn't be surprised to get to heaven and learn that Paul was actually stoned to death. He may very well have been raised from the dead by the disciples.

Either dead or near dead, he still walked thirty miles the next day. Most Christians could not walk thirty miles in a day if their life depended on it. I am not saying that to judge or condemn or to make anyone feel guilty or ashamed. I'm not trying to motivate you to start an exercise program or a walking program or a new diet. Those don't work. I am telling you that if you are devoted to God, you will quit indulging your flesh, not relying on your own strength. The desire to overeat will go away. I am telling you that if you will discern the body of Christ through the Lord's Supper, God will supernaturally heal your body and restore your health. God did it over and over again for Paul. He will do it for you. I am telling you that if you follow the Jesus Diet, you will be able to walk thirty miles in a day anytime you need to.

Here is the bottom line. What you are doing right now is not working. The teaching we have been given over the last twenty years is not working. Your self-efforts are not working. You are probably thinking it is your fault. You are right. It is your fault. You can't do it on your own. Trying to do it on your own is your fault. It won't work. What you do will not cut it. You can't do enough to change your health. What Christ did on the cross makes all of the difference. His body took all your sickness and disease off you, and He took them upon Himself. He was beaten and treated much more brutally than even Paul was. And it was on your behalf. He endured all the shame and brutality so you could walk in divine health. Doesn't that make you want to love Him? Doesn't that motivate you to serve Him? Doesn't devotion rise up inside of you when you think about what He did for you? That devotion is what will bring you divine health.

Even if you could do enough through your own self-efforts to lose weight or to get in better shape, you could never bring about divine health without God's help. You could never suffer the injuries Paul suffered on those two occasions and bounce back that quickly on your own. When you get a sickness or disease, the doctor rarely has a quick fix. If you get cancer, it is months of chemotherapy and radiation to just get to the point where you will hopefully survive. A full recovery takes months or years if it is even possible. You need all the resources that God provides for divine health. Jesus is the resource.

My business has what is called a trademark. It is actually registered with the government and is protected from theft. It is copyrighted, so no one else can use it. My business also has a name. That name has some protected rights. No one can use it for something similar without my permission. No one can use the name Google, Yahoo, or Facebook without their permission.

As a Christian, you have certain rights. You have the right to use the name of Jesus. Mark 16:17–18 says we have authority over the devil and demons must flee as we cast them out in His name. My business trademark and name are the identity of the business. In a similar way, you are identified as being in Christ. Your identity is wrapped up in Him. The Bible says we have become the righteousness of God in Christ. That is your identity.

The power of the Jesus Diet is found in the daily awareness of your identity. You are likely going to eat at least three meals a day, and you are going to drink something every day. Eating and sleeping are two things you do every day. God, in His wisdom, gave you instructions for those meals that would remind you to give thanks to God and to remember Christ. And you are rewarded with restored health and ongoing wellness. When you are devoted to Christ and expressing that devotion every day, miracles and health follow you just like they followed Paul.

I'm not saying to quit exercising if that is something you enjoy doing. If you like to run, then run to your heart's content. If you like to lift weights, go for it. Just don't rely on it. Don't think that your efforts are going to sustain you through your life. Devotion to God will make you stronger to endure life's struggles more than any weight-lifting program. Giving thanks expressing your devotion to God before you eat will leave you healthier than any diet you will ever try.

It all happens by faith. It is a free gift from God (grace) accessed by faith:

> For indeed the gospel was preached to us as well as to them; but the word which they heard did not profit them, not being mixed with faith in those who heard it. (Hebrews 4:2)

It did not profit them. Why? Because they did not mix it with faith. The gospel was preached to them, and they heard it, but they did not mix it with faith; therefore, it was of no profit. That is what this chapter is about. I want you to be doing things that profit you, not things that are of little to no value.

Diet and exercise are of little profit. Devotion to God is profitable for eternity and for this life. Thanking God before every meal with devotion is extremely profitable. Discerning the body of Christ is of great profit to you. Divine health is of great profit for living your life. You will be strong, vital, healthy, sickness-free, anxiety-free, rid of depression, pain-free, sorrow-free, and living life to the fullest.

That doesn't mean that bad things won't happen. They happened to Paul. Being stoned and beaten with rods is about as bad as it gets. It didn't stop Paul from doing what God called him to do. It didn't even take anything from his health. He was no worse for the wear. I am sure it was painful and hurt as it was happening, but he was as strong after enduring it as he had been before it even happened. Only God can do that. Only God can make you healthier by thanking him before a meal than someone who goes on the strictest diet. Only God can make you stronger and with more energy and vitality than a fitness guru.

CHAPTER 16
THE REST IS HISTORY

Come unto me, all ye that labour and are heavy laden, and I will give you rest. (Matthew 11:28 KJV)

God created us to need rest. Jesus often went away by Himself to a mountain to pray and to get away from the crowds and rest. God commanded in the ten commandments that man take an entire day each week and rest. There are tremendous health benefits to resting. Sleep is vital to health. It is when you are sleeping that your immune system kicks into gear and repairs your body of the stresses of the day. Studies have shown if you get more than seven hours of sleep every day, then you will have a lower risk of heart disease, cancer, obesity, and most other major diseases. In a previous chapter, we talked about the role of hunger and food.

It is actually when you are sleeping that your body produces leptin, which suppresses your appetite. When you don't get enough sleep, your body produces too much ghrelin, which is an appetite stimulant. Consequently, those who get less sleep tend to eat more, and those who get more sleep tend to regulate their food better. Getting enough sleep helps the Jesus Diet work better.

JESUS DIET PRINCIPLE #11
Jesus will give you rest.

However, Jesus is talking about more than just sleep when He said He will give us rest. The Greek word for "rest" means to calm or to ease. Jesus was saying He will ease and calm your fears and anxieties. Jesus knew how much you needed it. In America, one in five individuals is on an anti-anxiety or anti-depression medicine. One in four women is on mood-altering medications. The number of people on anti-anxiety medicines has increased by more than four hundred percent in the last two decades. If you are on those medications, I'm not trying to make you feel guilty or make you feel worse. It's just that fears and anxieties negate the effect of the Jesus Diet on your health. The Jesus Diet will help you get off those medications by helping you to overcome your fears.

As I mentioned earlier in the book, my wife and I have two little toy poodles, one boy and one girl. The boy weighs six pounds, and the girl weighs five and a half pounds. They are as gentle as they can be. We often walk them in the downtown area near where we live, and they always get a lot of attention. My wife dresses the girl in pink, and we get constant oohs and aahs. And our dogs play it for all its worth. When they hear someone make a comment, they stop in their tracks. They know someone thinks they are cute and is going to pet them. They love the attention so much they refuse to move until we stop and let the person dote on them.

Every time we walk, dozens of people stop and want to pet them, including small kids. One day, we encountered a couple walking with their eight-or nine-year-old daughter. As soon as she saw our dogs, she let out a blood-curdling scream. She was so petrified she had to be picked up and held until we could get away from her.

Her fear was totally irrational. Our dogs held no threat to her or to her safety. We would never let our dogs do anything to hurt her. Plus, our dogs weigh eleven pounds altogether. There is not much they could do to her. She could hurt them a lot worse than they could hurt her. Yet something inside of her created so much fear that she was in a state of panic. I felt bad for the little girl.

Fear is a natural reaction God gave us to respond to danger. If you see a bear in the woods, fear will motivate you to get away from it. However, fear is often not reality based. If you are walking in the woods and you hear a noise you think is a bear but is really a squirrel, you may feel fear, but it is not based on reality. The reality is there is nothing to be afraid of. You can't necessarily control the initial reaction of fear; however, what you do with the fear determines how it will manifest in your life and how it will affect your health.

Fear and anxiety can do tremendous damage to your health. Fear raises blood pressure and increases the risk of heart disease. Fear affects your digestive system. IBS (irritable bowel syndrome) is directly related to stress and anxiety. Fear, anxiety, and stress weaken your immune system and affect your sleep. Fear can trigger headaches, muscle pain, insomnia, and depression. Fear in a dangerous situation is normal. When fear becomes irrational, it can turn into a phobia if it persists for a long period of time. Not only will a phobia affect your health, but it can destroy the quality of your life.

A *phobia* is defined as an extreme or irrational fear. Researchers have come up with a phobia for almost everything. There is a phobia for the fear of the moon. Some people literally panic when they see the moon. In some severe cases, they will not even leave their house at night. There is a phobia for the fear of the northern lights. This is generally associated with people who visit where they can be seen. Many individuals have the equivalent of a panic attack when they see the lights. They must think aliens are in the lights, or something similar triggers the reaction.

I read about literally hundreds of phobias. There is a phobia for the fear of snow, mirrors, flying, bridges, flowers, ferns, birds, public speaking, getting married, wax museums, clowns, swallowing, going to church, speed, in-laws, injury, dogs, and doctors, to name a few. All of these have an actual medical name associated with the phobia.

Caligynephobia is the fear of beautiful women. I definitely don't have that phobia since I live with one. Gynophobia is the fear of women in general. I suppose all men have that one to some degree.

Aulophobia is the fear of flutes. My wife plays the flute. She plays in an ensemble with more than thirty women. They even have a few men in the group. Those men must not have gynophobia or aulophobia, or they wouldn't be able to stand being around that many women playing the flute!

There is basophobia which is the fear of walking or standing. Conversely, cathisophobia is the fear of sitting. I hope no one has both of these. What would he do?

There is porphyrophobia, which is the fear of the color purple. Cyanophobia is the fear of blue. Blue is my favorite color, and I am not sure why anyone would be afraid of it. Blue is supposed to be a calming and soothing color, and there is no reason to be afraid of it. Xanthophobia is the fear of yellow. Prasinophobia is the fear of green, chrysophobia is the fear of orange, and erythrophobia is the fear of red. I didn't find one for the fear of black. It would seem like that would be the scariest color.

Ablutophobia is the fear of bathing or showering. Those people are not too difficult to spot in the grocery store line. Genuphobia is the fear of knees. What is wrong with knees? I know some people find feet disgusting, but I've never heard that knees were something to fear. Jungliophobia is the fear of ankles.

Kaciraffphobia is the fear of ears. Someone must be making money every time they name a phobia. Why would you have to name a fear for every body part? We should have a fear of the person who has so much time on his hands to name all these phobias.

Aurephobia is the fear of gold. My wife definitely doesn't have that phobia. She loves anything made of gold. Is there a fear of diamonds? She doesn't have that fear either. Now that I think of it, I have never heard her express any fear related to the purchase of jewelry or purses. Or shoes for that matter.

Nomophobia is the fear of losing contact with your cell phone. Tell me about it! I think millions of people must have that one. Go anywhere, and everyone's on their phones. I've witnessed firsthand how some people react when they can't find their phone. It is utter panic. They can't stand the thought of being without their phone for even one minute.

Arithmophobia is the fear of numbers. I could have used this one during my high school algebra class. Maybe I could have gotten out of taking the tests if I had told them I had arithmophobia. Didaskaleinophobia is the fear of going to school. A lot more teenagers would claim to have that one if they were smart enough to spell it or pronounce it. Sesquipedalophobia is the fear of long words. That seems like kind of a cruel joke on someone who is suffering from it.

Dutchphobia is the fear of Dutch people. There is Sinophobia which is the fear of Chinese people. Francophobia is the fear of the French. Boshephobia is the fear of reading or hearing about the Bolsheviks. The Bolsheviks haven't been around since 1952! What is there to be afraid of? Walloonphobia is the fear of reading or hearing about the Walloons, who are a group of German-speaking people who live in Belgium. Apparently, they are very nice people that needn't be feared. Redneckaphobia is the fear of people from Arkansas. The fear of marrying your cousin or losing all your teeth at an early age is also a phobia related to the fear of people from Arkansas. (I just made those up).

Ephebiphobia is the fear of teenagers. I had three teenage boys at one time and that may not be such an irrational fear. I suffered from that for a dozen or so years. Pedophobia is the fear of little children or babies. My youngest son is getting married in a couple of months, and he expresses some of the symptoms of pedophobia when his fiancé talks about having children. I am glad that I now have a name for it.

Arachibutyrophobia is the fear of getting peanut butter stuck to the roof of your mouth. The fear is so strong in some people that they freak out when they see someone eating peanut butter. I remember as a kid trying to get it stuck to the roof of my mouth just for fun.

Phobophobia is the fear of phobias. I wonder if there is a fear of someone who doesn't have a phobia.

I'm not trying to make fun of those who suffer from these phobias. It's just that when you're reading about them, you can't help but realize how unnecessary and irrational they really are. I read a magazine article called "The 8 Things You Should Be Afraid Of." The premise of the article is that there are many things that we should legitimately be afraid of in life. There are so many things happening around us that could cause legitimate fear. Other drivers, for instance. Some people are such crazy drivers you have to be on the constant lookout for them. My son recently choked on a piece of steak, and his fiancé (the same one who wants kids), who is a nurse, did the Heimlich maneuver and saved his life. That could be a little scary while it is happening. There are some parts of town you definitely don't want to walk in at night.

Jesus said that we are not to be afraid of anything, even those things that seem dangerous. Read how Jesus reacted to a dangerous situation:

> On the same day, when evening had come, He said to them, "Let us cross over to the other side." Now when they had left the multitude, they took Him along in the boat as He was. And other little boats were also with Him. And a great windstorm arose, and the waves beat into the boat, so that it was already filling. But He was in the stern, asleep on a pillow. And they awoke Him and said to Him, "Teacher, do You not care that we are perishing?"
>
> Then He arose and rebuked the wind, and said to the sea, "Peace, be still!" And the wind ceased and there was a great calm.
> (Mark 4:35–39)

Jesus was asleep on the boat. He was not the least bit worried or affected by the storm. The disciples should not have been either. Notice in verse thirty-five that Jesus said, "Let's cross over to the other side." They should have had faith in those words. They were going to make it to the other side no matter how bad the storm was because Jesus said they would.

I wonder sometimes if God looks at us the same way we look at the little girl who was afraid of our dogs. I couldn't help but think how utterly silly it was to be afraid of two little poodles. God probably looks at our situation and how afraid and anxious we are with the same incredulity. Jesus couldn't understand why the disciples were freaking out. He probably didn't like being awakened from a good nap for no reason. Not that they were ever in any danger, but He immediately brought calm to the situation. The Bible says there was a "great calm." Would you like to have a "great calm" in your life? That is what Jesus can do for you. That is what He means when He says that He will give you rest. He will give you the ability to sleep in the midst of your storm. He will give you a great calm to endure your difficult circumstances.

Rest is a promise in the new covenant. Rest is part of grace. It is something Jesus is going to do for you. As we previously discussed, in the new covenant, the only way we can experience the promises of the new covenant is through faith. Rest comes by faith. Faith that our circumstances are under control is found in resting. Fear is the opposite of faith. Worry and anxiety counteract faith and negate faith in our lives. They create obstacles to our faith working. That is why Satan tries so hard to get us to express fear, worry, and anxiety. He knows it will keep us from the blessings God has for us. The Jesus Diet will not work without faith. Healing will not come without faith. Notice how Jesus talks about worry in relation to food:

> Therefore, I tell you, do not worry about your life, what you will eat or drink; (Matthew 6:25 NIV).

> So do not worry, saying, 'What shall we eat?' or 'What shall we drink?' or 'What shall we wear?' For the pagans run after all these things, and your heavenly Father knows that you need them. But seek first his kingdom and his righteousness, and all these things

will be given to you as well. Therefore do not worry about tomorrow, for tomorrow will worry about itself. Each day has enough
trouble of its own. (Matthew 6:31–34 NIV).

Most people worry about food. This passage is specifically speaking
about worrying about the provision of food, but I think it applies to
the way we worry about diets. Our society is obsessed with food and
diet. Most people think about food constantly. You are bombarded
with ads about food, diet, exercise, and weight loss. If you are on a
diet, you're thinking about that diet all day long. You are worrying
about what you are going to eat and how to keep from eating the
things not on your diet. When you mess up and break your diet, you
are worried about the guilt of having failed. Some people constantly
weigh themselves. That can easily become a manifestation of worry.
On the Jesus Diet, put the scales in the closet. You don't need them.
Trust and believe that God is going to help you to lose weight and
quit worrying about it.

If you are dealing with some physical sickness or disease, you are
probably constantly worrying about it. It can consume your life. Jesus said to not worry about anything, even those things that are
seemingly worrisome. He said He will give you rest. He will calm
the storm. He will bring you sleep even when it seems like your situation is hopeless. Even when you get a bad report from the doctor,
respond in faith and not fear. Your first response should be that you
will not accept the sickness. The report is wrong, or at least it is not
the entire story. It is not the destiny for your life.

Jesus died for your sicknesses and my diseases. He promised you
healing. That is your destiny. Therefore, whatever the doctor says is
not stronger than your faith or your God. Whatever fear your
friends or family express, rise above the storm and let Jesus bring
you a great calm. Don't listen to those voices of fear even if they are
from your best friends and family. The fear and anxiety will only
make the sickness worse anyway. Instead, choose by faith to con-

tinue to believe that giving thanks before each meal and discerning the body of Christ will bring healing to your body.

That is the power of the Jesus Diet. Every time you take in food, you are thinking about Jesus and what He did for you on the cross. You are thanking God for the provision of the food. But it is more than that. You are remembering that Jesus died for your healing. You are remembering all the promises Jesus has made to you in His word. You are remembering that He gives you rest. You are remembering how He gave the disciples a great calm in the midst of a storm. You are remembering how they made it safely to the other side just like He said they would.

When a financial problem comes up, every time you sit down to eat, remember Jesus told you not to worry about it. Remember the verse that says that God will supply all your needs. Don't rush into eating your food. Take time to think about God's promises for your difficult situations. If you have a bad report from the doctor, think about what the doctor said and then compare it to what God's word says. Say in faith, "This food is the body of Christ broken for me. My body is broken just as Jesus's body was broken. His was broken so mine doesn't have to be. By His stripes, I am healed. Because Jesus died for my healing, I refuse to worry. He will give me rest." Thank God for your healing even if it hasn't yet manifested. Every time you take a bite of food, remember it is the body of Christ that was broken for your healing. You remind yourself with every bite that you are healed in the name of Jesus.

Watch what happens. You will have peace. You will have rest. You will no longer be worried about your circumstances. Every bite increases your faith. With every bite, you are telling God you thank Him for His promises. You are thanking Him for the food and for the cup with the blood of Jesus, who died for your sins and your healing. You are releasing the power of the Lord's Supper into your body. The fears and anxieties will melt away.

Before you know it, you will be healed or at least at peace. It may happen instantly, or it may be over time. Keep believing until it manifests. If you are on medications, begin to confess and believe that you will no longer need them. If you are on anti-anxiety medicines, believe God will give you rest and pray that He will free you from your anxiety and fears to the point that you no longer need them. Anxiety and fear will leave and will be replaced with a great calm as you honor His body and blood.

At some point, you may not need the medicines. If you have to be on them until that time comes, pray for healing every time you take the Lord's Supper at your meal and ask God to heal whatever is in your body that is causing you to need them. Believe by faith that God is going to use the body of Christ to heal your body of anything that is abnormal in your body, including any imbalances that are causing the anxiety. Let the process of the Jesus Diet heal you of your need for those medications. I don't even like to call it the process of the Jesus Diet. It is not the diet. It is Jesus healing you. It is God who promised healing and Jesus who delivers the healing as you discern His broken body was for your healing.

You obviously need to take precautions when it comes to medications. You need to consult with your physician for a plan to wean yourself off the drugs if you can. They are very powerful drugs and change the chemical balance of your brain. Until God heals you completely, you may need them. You may not be able to just go off them cold turkey unless the Holy Spirit tells you to. God can heal you instantly. I have seen healings when the fear and anxiety were completely gone, and the person had no more need for medications. At the same time, use wisdom. You should get off them as God heals you and in the safest way possible. You will know by faith what you should do.

Anxiety and panic attacks run in my family. I have family members who get only a few hours of sleep at night because of their anxiety and make several trips to the emergency room a year because of panic attacks. One time, I was checking my blood pressure at the local grocery store and it was 180 over 110 for no reason. My blood pressure is normally perfect. I could feel that something was off, but I had no idea it was so high. I had a slight sinus issue, and I had taken a decongestant earlier in the day, and it turns out that was the culprit.

I went to the doctor, and he gave me a clean bill of health. He said the medication was what caused my blood pressure to spike. He gave me a blood pressure pill and anxiety medicine and said to take them if it should spike again. He said that once the medication was out of my system, the blood pressure would go back to normal.

Over the next few days, I didn't get any sleep. There was a battle in my mind. I knew nothing was wrong with me and that I was healed in the name of Jesus. I believed that by faith. At the same time, I had doubts. I struggled with wondering if something was actually wrong with me and that maybe something besides the decongestant was causing the blood pressure to spike.

I went to another doctor because my blood pressure would not go back to normal. At his office, my blood pressure was 194 over 114. By that time, the decongestant was out of my system, and the blood pressure was totally related to the anxiety. They were feeding on each other. The high blood pressure was because of the anxiety, and the anxiety was because of the blood pressure. The doctor said something very interesting. He said, "I am not the least bit worried about your blood pressure. I send people home all the time with blood pressure much higher than yours. It could be 230, and I would send you home because you don't have any symptoms of a heart attack or stroke. You are perfectly normal and healthy, and I think the anxiety is causing it." He prescribed me a different anti-anxiety medicine. I didn't need it. By the time I got back to my house, my blood pressure was normal, and I slept through the night.

The reason for this is because my mind was renewed to a new way of thinking. His words reassured me that nothing was wrong. It was like a switch went off in my mind, and my brain believed what the doctor said, that there was nothing to be worried about. My body responded by going back to normal.

That's what the Bible means when it says to renew your mind. Renewing your mind is believing the word of God. I believed the doctor. How much more should I believe God when He says I am healed by the stripes of Jesus? How much more should I believe Jesus when He said He would give me rest? How much more should I trust Him when He says to fear not?

Now, every time I eat food, I remember the word of God. Every time I take a drink of something, I remember the blood of Jesus that has covered all my sins. I believe Jesus when He says He will give me rest. I believe Him when He says that I don't have to worry about food. I believe when I thank God for my food before I eat it that God makes it good for me. I have seen it work firsthand in my life. I have seen sickness and disease miraculously leave my body. I have seen how thanking God for my food completely healed my digestive issues. I have heard thousands of testimonies from others who have been miraculously healed by the promises of God that have been accessed by faith.

Several years ago, I developed a pain in my back. It didn't go away, so I decided to go to the doctor. The doctor said I had shingles. I texted my wife from the doctor's office, and she texted back: "Oh No!" That was really encouraging! Donna had suffered from shingles several years before, and she said it was the most painful thing she had ever experienced. It had been on her neck and shoulder. She'd had to wear loose-fitting clothes because fabric irritated the severe rash she had developed. The doctor gave me two prescriptions and wanted to give me a shot. I told him I didn't want the shot, and I knew I wasn't going to fill the prescriptions. I knew I was going to be healed.

When I got home, my wife was very sympathetic. I told her not to worry about it because God had told me I was going to be healed by the following Tuesday and that it wouldn't be that bad. It was a Thursday, and Donna asked me why it would take five days. Why wasn't I just healed that day? I didn't have an answer, but I knew the Holy Spirit had told me I would be healed on Tuesday, and I believed it. Just like I believed what the doctor said about my blood pressure, I believed what the Holy Spirit said to me about Tuesday, even more so because He is God, and He actually knows the future.

I developed the severe rash that comes with shingles, but the pain never really bothered me. I just forgot about it and believed God was going to heal me on Tuesday. When Tuesday came, the rash started to fade. By Wednesday, it was completely gone. God had totally healed me of shingles in just five days! These types of manifestations of God healing me over the years and my seeing people healed when I prayed for them, have strengthened my faith to the point my natural response to sickness and disease is faith.

In the secular world, this is called systematic desensitization. It is the primary treatment for phobias. The concept was developed in the 1950s by Joseph Wolpe. He believed fear was a learned behavior; therefore, it could be unlearned. His idea was to gradually expose the patient to the fearful situation over time, increasing the exposure each time. He incorporated a relaxation process to help patients overcome their fears. Over time, they eventually overcame them without medication.

For instance, if a person is afraid of spiders, systematic desensitization slowly introduces the person to spiders in steps. Step one is to think about a spider. Step two is to look at a photo of a spider. Step three is to look at a live spider in a box. Step four is to hold the box. Step five is to let the spider out of the box and let it walk around the floor. Step six is to let it crawl on your shoe. Step seven is to let it crawl on your pants. Step eight is to let it crawl on your sleeve. Step nine is to let it crawl on your bare arm. Step ten is hold the spider in your hands. Once you can do that without fear, you are cured. Each step along the way, the person practices the relaxation techniques when the fear arises.

It's interesting how Wolpe associated overcoming fears with rest and relaxation. I don't know if he got that concept from God, but God said it first. That is how God said to overcome your fears: just rest. We don't even have to do the work of rest; God will do it for us.

Wolpe also determined that exposure to something will desensitize you to it so that it won't affect you anymore. Vaccines are based on that principle. The flu vaccine contains strains of the flu. When a small amount is injected into your body, your body becomes desensitized to it, and when the real strain hits, your body has built up the immunity to fight it off. When it comes to fears and phobias, facing them over a period of time eventually desensitizes you to them, and you are able to cope with them.

That is true in the spiritual as well as the physical realm. The more you rest and trust in God, over time, the more you are able to face your fears without worry and anxiety. I have seen God work so many miracles in my life that I am becoming desensitized to sickness and disease. When I have an unusual pain in my body, rather than becoming afraid, I speak to it and tell it to go away. Rather than being anxious, I rest. This is not something that you develop in a short time. It takes time to build the faith to respond properly to difficult circumstances.

Fear is a learned behavior that gets stronger over time. I believe fear is also from the enemy and many of the fears are not real and are to be resisted. For instance, I have two grandchildren, three months and three years old. My grandkids have no fear about the household finances. They don't ever worry about food. They just assume food is always going to be available. If my son lost his job and finances all the sudden became tight, my grandkids wouldn't know the difference. They just don't worry about it. They assume their father will take care of things. Jesus said we are to come to Him like little children:

And he said: "Truly I tell you, unless you change and become like little children, you will never enter the kingdom of heaven. (Matthew 18:3 NIV)

What Jesus meant was you are to accept Him at His word without worry and anxiety. You are to believe in Him with childlike faith. Just as my grandchildren don't worry about their next meal, neither should you. Just like they don't worry about their finances, you shouldn't either. If my grandkids get sick, they aren't worried about if they are going to die. They don't even know they should be worried about it.

Over time, you developed the learned behavior of fear. You learned that you can worry about finances, and you think you need to. You have seen how finances can create problems in your life. You know the devastating effects of illnesses and you have learned to fear them. That is why you need biblical desensitization. Biblical desensitization is exposing yourself to the word of God, then renewing your mind into believing the word, and then resting in it.

The Bible says we will have many troubles, but the Lord will deliver us from them all. Every time you face trouble and the Lord delivers you from it, it is an opportunity for you to become desensitized to trouble and fear. After many times of seeing the Lord deliver you from trouble, eventually, those fears will go away completely.

There is also a secular technique called flooding that is also used to overcome phobias. Flooding is extreme and prolonged exposure to a fearful situation. The patient is overexposed to their fears all at once. The extreme exposure helps them to get over them right away. It is like ripping off a Band-Aid. Get it over quickly so the pain is not prolonged. Isaiah says:

When the enemy shall come in like a flood, the Spirit of the Lord shall lift up a standard against him. (Isaiah 59:19 KJV)

The enemy may not let you have the time to be desensitized. He may come in like a flood. Your first response may be extreme fear. Have you ever heard the saying "Fight fire with fire?" That is what the Holy Spirit does. The enemy comes in like a flood, and the Holy Spirit will lift up a standard against him. The Holy Spirit will fight your battle for you and match Satan, fiery dart with fiery dart, and none will hurt you. If you understand that, you will not be afraid.

Seeing the Holy Spirit deliver you from those situations time and time again builds your faith to the point where your natural reaction is to trust God. That is what I mean by biblical desensitization. Eventually, you will come to the point that nothing will bother you, just like some can come to the point when they can pick up a spider and it won't bother them.

When the disciples were on the boat and the severe storm was raging, their natural response was fear. They woke Jesus, petrified. Jesus said, "Where is your faith?" Then He said, "Don't you remember how I fed the multitudes?" He reminded them of how He can work any miracle and that they have nothing to fear. He tried to point to their successes to realize that they could trust in Him.

That's what the Jesus Diet will do for you. Every time you take a bite of food, you are remembering what Christ did for you, and you are thanking God for it. You remember the moments of fear and how God came through in those situations. You remember that you don't have to be worried about sickness and disease. Jesus died for those sicknesses, and the bread that you are eating is His body that was broken for you. Over time, your body will become desensitized to fear, worry, and anxiety about sicknesses.

This is a very powerful principle that will change your life. Jesus told the disciples to remember the past. Remember the times that God was faithful to them. If they had remembered the past, they would not have been worried about the future. The title of this chapter is "The Rest Is History." You can rest in your future knowing your history.

CHAPTER 17
THE FOUNTAIN OF YOUTH

Who satisfies your desires with good things
so that your youth is renewed like the eagle's. (Psalm 103:5 NIV)

Since the beginning of time, man has sought immortality. In the Garden of Eden, Satan tempted Adam and Eve to eat of the fruit by saying God had lied and they would not really die if they ate from it. They thought eating the fruit might allow them to live forever like God. They didn't realize God had already given them immortality as long as they didn't eat the fruit. They did the exact opposite of what would have prolonged their lives. Since then, man has been doing the exact opposite of what he should be doing to prolong his life. Many futile attempts to achieve immortality have actually ended in premature death.

Qin Shi Huang was the first emperor of the Chinese Qin dynasty. There were three assassination attempts on his life, and he lived in constant fear of dying. He was so afraid of death he became obsessed with finding a formula that would help him live forever. He had a number of alchemists working on a formula, and he tested several of them. One of the formulas contained mercury, and Huang died after drinking it at only forty-nine years of age. Five other Qin emperors died after drinking the same or similar formulas.

Alexander Bogdanov was a Russian physician. He believed the key to immortality was in blood transfusions. He did eleven such transfusions on himself by exchanging blood with other patients. He would inject younger patients' blood into himself and inject his blood into them. He noted that his eyesight improved and his balding stopped, and he documented several other positive health changes from the transfusions. Until his last one. He exchanged blood with a student suffering from malaria and tuberculosis. He suffered a very slow and painful death.

Many Buddhist monks have attempted to achieve immortality by a practice known as self-mummification. They were basically buried alive. Leading up to the procedure, the monk ate a special diet and drank an embalming solution. They were encased inside a burial chamber that was sealed until they died. The belief was that the monk was not dead; he was just in a meditative state and would wake up one day and re-enter the world with his mind and body intact. Too bad they were wrong. They are all dead. They know now that it wasn't such a good idea.

The philosopher's stone is a legendary substance that supposedly turns mercury into gold when it is consumed. It was called the "elixir of life" and had purported properties of rejuvenation and, ultimately, immortality. Unfortunately, many have died drinking and handling the substance. Sir Isaac Newton was said to have developed mercury poisoning from working on the formula. In his last days, he suffered tremors, confusion, delusions, insomnia, and dementia. He should have stuck with math and astronomy. Those are much safer.

Henry II of France's mistress, Diane De Poitiers, died prematurely after drinking a concoction of gold. It was said she was a woman of striking beauty, which she maintained most of her life. She might've been the most beautiful woman alive at that time. Her attempts to maintain that beauty resulted in her premature death as tests show her hair had gold poisoning from drinking the potion. Gold is to be worn, not drunk. That should be every woman's motto.

Cryogenic freezing is the process of attempting to preserve a dead body by freezing it in liquid nitrogen with the hopes of someday warming the body and bringing the person back to life. Here is how the process works. Freezing must begin shortly after the patient dies to prevent brain damage. The body is cooled in an ice bath, slowly reducing its temperature. In some cases, doctors administer ongoing CPR to try and prevent brain cells from dying. They drain the body of all its blood and inject antifreeze into the body to prevent ice crystals from forming. That makes sense. You don't want ice crystals forming in your body. That couldn't be good.

You can go a cheaper route and only have your head frozen. That is only $80,000 as opposed to preserving your whole body, which costs a whopping $200,000. Either way, the company makes out like a bandit because they will never have the cost that is budgeted for the recovery since it will never happen. No need to be frozen. Every person will be resurrected by Jesus on the last day. One man actually paid for the services and then shot himself the same day so he could ensure he would be frozen immediately. Unfortunately, the bullet did so much damage he reduced the likelihood that he will ever be able to be rejuvenated, not that he had any chance anyway. The website now has instructions on how to kill yourself if you want to be preserved.

Pud Galvin was a major league baseball pitcher in the nineteenth century. He is a member of the Hall of Fame and won more than three hundred games. He is the first player who admitted to using performance-enhancing drugs. He drank what he called a miracle substance that contained monkey testosterone. He had a good career, but he did not obtain immortality. He died at age forty-five from "catarrh of the stomach." It is a painful way to die and the sufferer's breath becomes "an excessively fetid and sickening odor, so offensive as to render the patient an object of disgust to himself as well as to others." That must have hindered his ability to parlay his celebrity into dates.

Researchers have found that severe calorie restriction increases longevity. A monkey was started on a severe calorie restriction diet when he was sixteen years old, and he has lived to the ripe old age of forty-three which is equivalent to man living 130 years. They tested the restricted diets on humans, but they had such a high dropout rate they couldn't get an accurate measure of its results. The only conclusion they could come to was that the diet probably makes you live longer, but it also makes life not worth living.

All these attempts at immortality are a waste of time. I have already achieved immortality. I'm going to live forever, and I don't have to be mummified, frozen, or drink any deadly concoction. Here is what Jesus said:

And whoever lives and believes in Me shall never die. Do you believe this? (John 11:26)

I believe in Jesus, and I will never die. I wish all those people in the above examples had only known this truth. It would have saved them money and would have extended their lives on this earth. You don't have to pay $80,000 or $200,000 to have your body frozen. Save the money. Give it to the church. You just have to believe in Jesus, and you will live for an eternity with Him:

For we know that if our earthly house, this tent, is destroyed, we have a building from God, a house not made with hands, eternal in the heavens. For in this we groan, earnestly desiring to be clothed with our habitation which is from heaven, if indeed, having been clothed, we shall not be found naked. For we who are in this tent groan, being burdened, not because we want to be unclothed, but further clothed, that mortality may be swallowed up by life. Now He who has prepared us for this very thing is God, who also has given us the Spirit as a guarantee.

So we are always confident, knowing that while we are at home in the body we are absent from the Lord. For we walk by faith, not by sight. We are confident, yes, well pleased rather to be absent from the body and to be present with the Lord. (2 Corinthians 5:1–8)

"Absent the body is present with the Lord." There is never a moment when you're dead. Your body becomes of no use to you, and it quits breathing, for sure, but the moment it does, if you are a believer, you come into the presence of Jesus. I am convinced most Christians don't really believe this. If they did, why would they be so afraid of dying? Why are we so fearful of everything? Why are we trying so hard to live longer if dying is better because we will be with Jesus immediately?

Paul said it was far better to go and be with Christ (Philippians 1:23). He said that he remained in his body for their benefit. He still had things to accomplish for God, so he was willing to stay on this earth even though it would be far better to go and be with Jesus:

For I am hard-pressed between the two, having a desire to depart and be with Christ, which is far better. Nevertheless to remain in the flesh is more needful for you. (Philippians 1:23–24)

It's better to go and be with Jesus, but you need to stay on this earth to accomplish what God has for you. Many Christians search for a longer life through medical procedures, fad diets, magic pills, elixirs, and prescription drugs because they are afraid of dying. Even more Christians make every attempt possible to look younger through Botox injections, plastic surgery, liposuction, breast augmentation, miracle creams, and every imaginable new fad, hoping to combat the natural aging process. Those are unnecessary. You want to be healthy, and you want to look your best and there is nothing wrong with that. The reason is the problem. You should want to be healthy and look your best so you can fulfill God's plan for your life, not because you are afraid of dying or so vain that you can't stand the fact that you are aging.

Even if you have the right motive, you are probably using the wrong methods. Trying to extend your life through diet and exercise is the wrong approach as well. Did you know that longevity and youthfulness are promises in the Bible? So, what exactly prolongs your life? Proverbs 10:27 tells us:

The fear of the Lord prolongs days.

The "fear of the Lord" is a Jewish expression. It doesn't mean we are afraid of God. The fear of the Lord means we worship Him. It is an attitude of awe, reverence, adoration, and love. That is what I have been saying in this book. Eating the right diet or exercising four to five days a week is not the answer to a prolonged life. There is nothing wrong with those things. They are of some benefit, but it is a limited benefit. Worship of God prolongs days. Do you want to live a long life? Live a life of worship and adoration of God. Honor God with your food. Give thanks to Him before every meal. Remember the body of Christ and how it was broken for you and remember the blood that was shed for you. Don't just remember them; worship and thank Jesus for them.

Don't rely on your self-efforts of diet and exercise. That is an affront to God. That is, you saying to God, that you don't need Him. You believe you can extend your life yourself through your own ideas. Those vain attempts will lead you to nothing but pain and suffering. Let God satisfy you with a long life:

With long life I will satisfy him,

And show him My salvation. (Psalm 91:16)

God will satisfy you with a long life. Not only will you live a long time, but you will be satisfied. Are you satisfied now with your own self-efforts? What does God show him that will satisfy him? "My salvation." The Hebrew word for salvation is "Yesha." Jesus's Hebrew name is Yeshua, which means "the Lord is salvation." God will satisfy you with a long life by showing you Jesus. He is your salvation. He is the source of your long life. So, what does Jesus show us about salvation? Jesus said that you can't add one hour or minute to your life through your own efforts:

> Therefore I tell you, do not worry about your life, what you will eat or drink; or about your body, what you will wear. Is not life more than food, and the body more than clothes? Look at the birds of the air; they do not sow or reap or store away in barns, and yet your heavenly Father feeds them. Are you not much more valuable than they? Can any one of you by worrying add a single hour to your life? (Matthew 6:25–27 NIV)

You can't even add one hour to your life, so quit trying. Quit trying to do it on your own. Quit worrying about your life. Quit worrying about food and drink. Quit worrying about wrinkles. You can't add a single hour to your life by worrying. The only thing you can do is to honor God and believe you will receive a long life through His grace and mercy.

I've read hundreds of diets and exercise plans promise amazing results, including longevity. I've purposefully avoided personal illustrations in this book. I have not added very many success stories and personal testimonies. I have not told you all the many ways the Jesus Diet has impacted my life. I don't want you to be convinced that the Jesus Diet will transform your health because it did it for me or for someone else. I don't want to put a "before and after" picture in this book so you might have hope it will work for you. Your hope must be in Jesus, not in a process or a plan. Those plans need those seemingly fantastic success stories because they don't work.

Have you ever watched the show The Biggest Loser? A study of season eight found that the results may not be what you think. The winner of season eight lost a whopping 239 pounds in seven months. He started the program weighing 440 pounds. After winning, he was on all the television shows touting the success of the program.

He is quoted as saying, "I've got my life back. I feel like a million bucks." Since then, he has gained back more than a hundred pounds and most of the other sixteen contestants gained all their weight back as well, and many actually weigh more than when they started the show.

I don't want you to do the Jesus Diet because someone else says they lost one hundred pounds on it. I don't want you to do the Jesus Diet because someone else was healed from their sickness and diseases. I want you to do the Jesus Diet because you are convinced it is what God wants you to do. I want you to be convinced because of what the word of God says, not because it worked for me.

JESUS DIET PRINCIPLE #12
Honor God, and He will lengthen your days and make them enjoyable and renew your youth like the eagles.

Ephesians 6:2–3 (NIV) tells you how to live a long life:

> Honor your father and mother—which is the first commandment with a promise— so that it may go well with you and that you may enjoy long life on the earth.

"Honor your father and mother and you may live long on the earth." That promise has nothing to do with diet or exercise. It doesn't say: "Eat healthy and exercise four to five times a week, and you will enjoy a long life on earth." It says to simply honor your father and mother and if you do, things will go well for you on this earth, and you will enjoy a long life. Notice it says that not only will you live a long life, but you will enjoy a long life:

> He asked you for life, and you gave it to him—
> **length of days**, for ever and ever.
> Through the victories you gave, his glory is great;
> you have bestowed on him splendor and majesty.

> Surely you have granted him unending blessings
> and made him glad with the joy of your presence.
> For the king trusts in the Lord;
> through the unfailing love of the Most High
> he will not be shaken. (Psalm 21:4–7 NIV)

How would you like to live a length of days and have unending blessings for all those days? Trust in the Lord, then (v.7). It is through the "unfailing love of the Most High" that your days will be lengthened, and your blessings will overflow.

King Solomon had a dream and here is what God told him in 1 Kings 3:14 NIV:

> And if you walk in obedience to me and keep my decrees and commands as David your father did, I will give you a long life."

Notice the old covenant language. If you will keep my commandments, then you will have a long life. That was conditional. That was how the old covenant worked. Obey God, and God would bless you. The new covenant has the same promises only better. The new covenant is based on faith. Believe in Jesus, and God will give you a long life. Notice that a long life is a free gift. That is grace. Even in the old covenant, the blessings of God were gifts. You can't create a long life on your own. It is a free gift from God. There is no magic pill or potion you can take that will increase your days. Only God can give you a long life. While God is giving you a long life through grace, He will also do something remarkable: He will renew your youth. Here is what it says in Psalm 103:5:

> Who satisfies your mouth with good things,
> So that your youth is renewed like the eagle's.

God will renew your youth like the eagle's youth is renewed. Have you ever seen an eagle? He flies nonstop. He has unending energy. You can't tell an old eagle from a young eagle. They both soar with the wind. Eagles also molt annually. Every year, they shed their old and used feathers and grow new ones. An eagle has 7,200 feathers, so it is quite a process. God is constantly renewing their youth!

Did you know your body is constantly being renewed? There are between fifty and seventy-five trillion cells in your body. Each cell has its own lifespan. Red blood cells live for about four months, and white blood cells for about a year. Skin cells live for two to three weeks. Colon cells die off about every four days. God is renewing your youth every few days. Your attitude towards God affects the success of the renewal.

God promised Solomon a long life if he kept the commandments as part of the old covenant. The Bible says Solomon didn't keep the commandments and married foreign wives. Those foreign wives turned his heart away from God. Solomon died prematurely. His father, David, lived a long life because he was a man after God's own heart. David wasn't perfect. David committed the horrible sins of adultery and murder, but he still lived a long life. It was because he honored God. Solomon turned his heart away from God and lived fifty fewer years even though he had more money, wisdom, wives, and possessions. He did not follow the instructions on how to have a long life.

In the new covenant, the length of your life is not based on keeping the commandments. It is based on the extent to which you honor God. The grace of God for long life and abundant life is accessed by faith. Honor God, and your youth is renewed. Honor God, and He satisfies your mouth with good things. I wonder if that in part is a reference to food? God will give you food that satisfies, and while He is giving you pleasant food to eat that is satisfying, He will renew your youth. Look at the verses leading up to God renewing your youth like the eagle's:

> Bless the Lord, O my soul;
> And all that is within me, bless His holy name!
> Bless the Lord, O my soul,

And forget not all His benefits:
Who forgives all your iniquities,
Who heals all your diseases,
Who redeems your life from destruction,
Who crowns you with lovingkindness and tender mercies,
Who satisfies your mouth with good things,
So that your youth is renewed like the eagle's. (Psalm 103:1–5)

The Psalmist starts by blessing the Lord. With everything within him, he blessed the holy name of the Lord. That is the beginning of renewing your youth. But also forget not all His benefits. What are His benefits in verse three? He forgives you your sins, and He heals all your diseases! That is the Lord's Supper. The Psalmist said to not forget; Jesus said to remember. Same thing. What are you not supposed to forget, and what are you supposed to remember? Your benefits. What are your benefits? The blood of Christ that forgives all your iniquities and the body of Christ that heals all your diseases.

What is the end result? He "redeems your life from destruction, crowns you with lovingkindness and tender mercies, satisfies your mouth with all good things, and renews your youth like the eagle."

JESUS WILL RENEW YOUR YOUTH LIKE THE EAGLE'S

My friend, only God can renew your youth like the eagles. You don't need to try to do it yourself. You don't need plastic surgery to look younger. Let God renew your youth. The emperors of China couldn't discover it. Ironically, they died early trying to reach immortality. The very thing they hoped would extend their life actually took their lives early. The greatest alchemists that ever lived haven't been able to create a potion that will extend life.

Billions are spent every year on anti-aging research, and nothing has been discovered that can significantly increase life expectancy.

A well-known entrepreneur recently died of pancreatic cancer with a net worth of more than ten billion dollars. His money couldn't save him. He was actually a vegan. His supposedly healthy diet didn't prevent him from getting cancer. I wouldn't be surprised if we someday learn that it contributed. Have you not yet learned that the ways of the world don't bring happiness and good health? It is said that when he learned he had cancer, he immediately started a regimen of alternative health supplements and diets to try and cure himself. The doctors said it actually caused him to die earlier than he would have if he hadn't tried anything. Did I also mention that he was a Buddhist? Isaiah tells us the secret to health:

> But they that wait upon the Lord shall renew their strength; they shall mount up with wings as eagles; they shall run, and not be weary; and they shall walk, and not faint. (Isaiah 40:31 KJV)

The Lord shall "renew your strength." How would you like to have strength renewed by the Lord? You will run and not get weary. You will walk and not faint. You will live a long life full of vitality and energy. That is the life that I want.

I know. Some Christians die early. I'm convinced most die prematurely because they are not giving thanks before their meals and not discerning the body of Christ with every meal. I am praying that this book will go viral through the body of Christ and transform how we approach food and drink. Even so, children will die of tragic diseases, and they might never have the chance to learn to give thanks and to discern the body of Christ. Christians die every day from persecution, car wrecks, murders, and accidents. This book won't change that reality. Those things often make us question God and His goodness. Why? It is because we don't believe what Paul said: "Absent the body is present with the Lord." What could be better than that? Though we should grieve the loss of the time with our loved one, if we really believed what Paul said, we would be happy for the one who got to go be with the Lord.

Does that mean we should all want to die prematurely? By no means! We should want to live to fulfill God's will and desire for our lives. I want to live so my grandkids hear about Jesus. I want to live to write more books and teach and preach a message of grace to this generation. I want to outlive my wife, so she never has to live as a widow. But I want to enjoy my days. I want them to be long and prosperous, and I want to be in good health. I want to run the race without fainting and without growing weary. I want God to renew my youth so that, all my days, I have the same energy and vitality I had when I was a teenager.

I'm convinced that honoring God will get me there. I am convinced the principles of the Jesus Diet will prolong my days on this earth and my youth will be renewed like the eagles. Someday, I will get to go be with the Lord and hopefully hear the words: "Well done, my good and faithful servant."

CONCLUSION
OUR DAILY BREAD

But without faith it is impossible to please Him, for he who comes
to God must believe that He is, and that He is a rewarder of those
who diligently seek Him. (Hebrews 11:6)

Man loves to give himself awards. There are music awards, sports
awards, movie awards, science awards, and acting awards along with
many others. I looked on Wikipedia, and there are thousands of
awards. Really, how many different country music awards do we
need? I don't think these awards made the list:

The National Odor-Eaters Rotten Sneaker Contest is held annually in New York. Last year was the forty-fourth year and open to
children between the ages of five and fifteen. It's a national competition with a series of local contests held around the United States.
Shoes are judged on odor, condition, and an explanation from the
child as to why his or her sneakers are the stinkiest. They probably
have a hard time getting judges for that contest!

There is the Stella Award, which goes annually to the person who
filed the dumbest lawsuit the previous year. A fifty-seven-year-old
law student from Washington, DC, won for filing a lawsuit against
his dry cleaner. Allegedly, they lost a pair of his pants, and he sued
them for $65,462, 500. Those must have been some special pants.
Were they a family heirloom? He must have claimed emotional dis-

tress. Sadly, he lost the case. The judge ruled he didn't have a pant leg to stand on! I made that up.

There are six Nobel Prizes, including awards for scientific advancements. There is the IG Nobel Prize, not affiliated with the real one, that gives an award each year for the worst scientific achievement. A winner in medicine received the award for his study of the side effects of sword swallowing. He determined that the primary side effect is a sore throat! A winner in linguistics studied rats. He determined that rats could not tell the difference between a person speaking Japanese backwards from a person speaking Dutch backwards. Really, how could you possibly know either way? And if a rat could tell the difference, what exactly would that prove? I'm hoping that person didn't use taxpayer money for that study.

There are six different awards for the worst movie of the year. I have a few nominations for them, and that must be a hard one to judge as well. There are so many to choose from. How could you possibly choose the worst one? I looked at the list of winners hoping I had not seen a single one on the list. I made it through a lot of the list until I saw that the 2003 winner was From Justin to Kelly. I saw that one but only because my wife made me. To her credit, she thought it was one of the worst movies ever made as well.

There's the annual award for the dumbest statement made by a public figure. It is called the Foot-in-Mouth Award. Two people have won it more than once. You would think once would be enough. Naomi Campbell won one year for this line: "I love England. Especially the food. There is nothing I love more than a lovely bowl of pasta." Richard Gere won for "I know who I am. No one else knows who I am. If I was a giraffe and somebody said I was a snake, I'd think, 'No, actually I am a giraffe.'" Alicia Silverstone described her views on her movie Clueless: "I think that Clueless was very deep. I think it was deep in the way that it was very light. I think lightness has to come from a very deep place if it's true lightness." I wonder if Clueless also won the worst movie award? I hope not because I saw that one with my wife as well. I don't want to have seen two movies on the list. Jessica Simpson did not win the award, but she should have when she argued, "Chicken of the Sea is chicken! It's not tuna!"

When I watch these award shows, I can't help thinking that man really likes to pat himself on the back. God is a rewarder and we are made in his image. Maybe that's where we get it from. God has been rewarding man since the beginning of time. I'm not sure it's as much that He is a rewarder as it is that He just loves to bless us. He is looking for every opportunity to bless those who seek Him. Solomon was the richest man who ever lived. Job was described as "the greatest man in all the east" (Job 1:3). He achieved that status because he was "blameless and upright." God has always found ways to abundantly bless His people.

God attached an award to giving thanks before your meal and discerning the Lord's body. The reward is divine health. It is interesting to me that God attached divine health in the new covenant to eating meals. I think it is because you eat three meals a day. It's the thing that you do most consistently. The purpose of giving thanks before a meal and discerning the Lord's body at each meal is so you take time each day to remember Christ and to honor God for His provision of food. At least three times a day, you are taking time out to think about God.

When Jesus taught us how to pray, He even mentioned food:

Our Father in heaven,
Hallowed be Your name.
Your kingdom come.
Your will be done
On earth as it is in heaven.
Give us this day our daily bread.
(Matthew 6:8–11)

Even when we pray, we should be remembering God is the one who provides us with our daily bread. We should be thanking God as we sit down to eat our food, and we should be always mindful of the body and blood of Christ.

The basic premise of the Jesus Diet is that food is not about us. We have made it about us satisfying our flesh. Food is about honoring God. It's also about something else. Food is to be used as an act of service:

Jesus said if you give away food God has blessed you with, He will repay you:

> Then He also said to him who invited Him, "When you give a dinner or a supper, do not ask your friends, your brothers, your relatives, nor rich neighbors, lest they also invite you back, and you be repaid. But when you give a feast, invite the poor, the maimed, the lame, the blind. And you will be blessed, because they cannot repay you; for you shall be repaid at the resurrection of the just." (Luke 14:12-14)

You don't give away your food so you will be rewarded. You give away your food because you are actually doing it for Christ:

> For I was hungry and you gave me something to eat, I was thirsty and you gave me something to drink, I was a stranger and you invited me in, I needed clothes and you clothed me, I was sick and you looked after me, I was in prison and you came to visit me.

> "Then the righteous will answer him, 'Lord, when did we see you hungry and feed you, or thirsty and give you something to drink? When did we see you a stranger and invite you in, or needing clothes and clothe you? When did we see you sick or in prison and go to visit you?'"

> "The King will reply, 'Truly I tell you, whatever you did for one of the least of these brothers and sisters of mine, you did for me.'" (Matthew 25:35–40 NIV)

That really is the essence of the Jesus Diet. Food is about something more than how good it tastes. It's more than satisfying your cravings. It's about eating to live, eating to honor God, and eating to serve others. In serving others, you are serving Christ:

> Whatever you do, work at it with all your heart, as working for the Lord, not for human masters, since you know that you will receive an inheritance from the Lord as a reward. It is the Lord Christ you are serving. (Colossians 3:23–24 NIV)

Turn your focus away from your self-effort and your use of food to gratify your desires and turn your focus to serving Christ. You will receive an inheritance from the Lord as a reward. Every act of service is service to Christ. Imagine how your life would change if your focus was honoring God through your meals and serving Christ through your eating.

The disciples were so blessed. Imagine what it must have been like to eat almost every meal with Jesus for three years. What would it have been like to eat the Lord's Supper with Jesus in the upper room that night? I can imagine them sitting around the table, listening to Jesus tell stories and teaching them about God. I can imagine them sitting around a campfire, cooking fish caught that day, laughing and having a great time.

You can have that same experience every time you sit down to eat. You can eat your meals with Jesus. You can partake of the Lord's Supper with Him just like the disciples did. Like Jesus, begin the meal by thanking God for the food. Then remember what Jesus did on the cross. Be mindful of what Jesus is saying to you through the Holy Spirit. Jesus will give you instructions on what to eat and drink and what to do in every area of your life. Every time you break bread, you are having a meal with Him. Someday, you will be eating with Him in person:

> Assuredly, I say to you, I will no longer drink of the fruit of the vine until that day when I drink it new in the kingdom of God. (Mark 14:25)

Jesus made that statement the night of the Lord's Supper. What a glorious day that will be! In the meantime, remember Him at each meal and take every opportunity to provide food to the poor.

This is my twenty-second book. I have enjoyed writing this as much as any I have written before. It's my privilege to write it for you. I pray this book brings restoration to your health and draws you closer to God. I love that the focus of this book is Jesus. He said of Himself that no one comes to the Father but through Him. If I have pointed you to Jesus, then I have done what I set out to do.

PRINCIPLES OF JESUS DIET

1. Jesus made all foods clean.

2. You can eat anything you want.

3. Always say a prayer of thanksgiving before you eat, and the food and drink will become consecrated and beneficial for your body.

4. Honor the body of Christ often.

5. Partaking of the Lord's Supper often, helps to maintain your closeness to Christ.

6. Jesus came to provide spiritual and physical healing.

7. Listen to the Holy Spirit. It is Jesus speaking to you, giving you instructions on how to have an abundant life.

8. Let God change you on the inside, and your outward appearance will change as well.

9. Eat when you are hungry; quit when you are full.

10. Pursue those things that really profit you.

11. Jesus will give you rest.

12. Honor God and He will lengthen your days and make them enjoyable and renew your youth like eagles.

Free Online Resources at
www.terrytoler.com

Published by Beholdings Publishing

Made in the USA
Las Vegas, NV
29 January 2022

42566618R00152